# BROWN
# GIRL
# LIKE ME

# BROWN GIRL LIKE ME

## JASPREET KAUR

bluebird
books for life

First published 2021 by Bluebird

This paperback edition first published 2023 by Bluebird
an imprint of Pan Macmillan
The Smithson, 6 Briset Street, London EC1M 5NR
*EU representative:* Macmillan Publishers Ireland Ltd, 1st Floor,
The Liffey Trust Centre, 117–126 Sheriff Street Upper,
Dublin 1, D01 YC43
Associated companies throughout the world
www.panmacmillan.com

ISBN 978-1-5290-5635-8

9 8 7 6 5 4 3 2 1

A CIP catalogue record for this book is available from the British Library.

Typeset in Minion Pro by Palimpsest Book Production Limited, Falkirk, Stirlingshire
Printed and bound by CPI Group (UK) Ltd, Croydon, CR0 4YY

Visit **www.panmacmillan.com/bluebird** to read more about all our books
and to buy them. You will also find features, author interviews and
news of any author events, and you can sign up for e-newsletters
so that you're always first to hear about our new releases.

# CONTENTS

# INTRODUCTION

## *Seen and Unseen*

Sundays would always mean one thing in my house when I was a kid. Hair-wash day. This ritual is probably one of my earliest memories, me sitting at my mum's feet whinging as every knot passed through the comb, followed by a generous amount of coconut oil being rubbed into my head and finished off with a nice, neat plait. This precious time with my mum was a mixture of haircare and storytime. Whilst she nourished my little head and stimulated the blood circulation, Mum would share stories about her childhood, memories of how my grandma would do the same thing for her every Sunday back in their *pind* near Jalandhar, Punjab. A precious time when women caught up, shared worries and connected to their roots. Literally. But one day, after one of my first days of high school, I stormed home and screamed at my mum to never put oil in my hair again.

Earlier that day, I was unpacking textbooks into my locker out of the huge backpack Dad and I bought from Barking market a few weeks earlier. I say huge because it literally felt like a suitcase, the kind of backpack that (as my brother kindly noted) made me look like a Teenage Mutant Ninja Turtle. It even had wheels . . . Anyway, as I neatly arranged my lovely new

1

sticky-back-plastic-covered books in my locker, I could hear a group of girls sniggering behind me. 'Yeah, she always stinks of curry!' They were referring to the smell of *tarka* coming from the blazer that I had left in the kitchen the night before. A smell that no amount of Impulse body spray could mask. 'And her hair is so greasy, doesn't she ever wash it!?' I could feel my cheeks burning with embarrassment. I pretended I couldn't hear them and decided not to turn around. With a snigger and shove, the girls howled with laughter and walked away. That's why from that day, and to my mum's heartbreak, I didn't want to oil and plait my hair ever again.

The act of oiling hair was a bond formed between generations of brown women. The use of natural vegetable oils to nourish both hair and skin has been documented for over 5,000 years in South Asia. I don't think it's a coincidence that in Sanskrit, the word *sneha* means 'to oil' but also 'to love' or give affection. It makes complete sense to me now, the loving act of oiling and nourishing yourself. Fast forward to the present day, and it's become an essential part of my self-care Sunday routine, which I now prefer to call 'hair-wash-Sunday'.* But why was I so ashamed of something embedded in my culture and roots for such a long time? Is this where I started to internalize some kind of self-hate towards my identity and being a brown girl?

I never recognized my brownness or 'otherness' before this point. My family and I grew up in east London, and like anyone who speaks of their hometown fondly, I would say it was a really

* [*hair-wash-Sunday*, noun; the day of the week before Monday and after Saturday, dedicated to self-care. This includes, but is not limited to, washing your hair, applying oil, body scrubs, use of face masks, meditating and resting before the week ahead]

special place. When my grandad (Babaji) first came to the UK in the early 1960s, he decided to settle in the East End, moving around from Greenwich to Newham and eventually Ilford. I was born in Barking Hospital, something that my husband always reminds me of every time 'ting from Barking' comes on the radio. The world that I saw, the world that I knew, felt like Ilford Lane, Southall Broadway or Soho Road. In that bubble, I went to school with kids from all walks of life. I grew up with brown friends, black friends, white friends, Jamaicans, Somalis, Turkish, Bengali and Punjabi, and all kinds of communities – Jewish, Muslim, Sikh, Hindu, you name it. I had Catholic friends and Sunni and Shia friends. White working-class kids ate their packed lunch with brown working-class kids. As a brown girl navigating these spaces, I may have faced some social and cultural barriers which we'll come back to shortly, but at least I felt part of the world I knew; normal even. This was the London I knew.

But somewhere in the time between childhood and adolescence I began to deny all of the beautiful parts of what make me a brown girl. I looked around for role models to look up to, or for someone who had gone through these struggles before, but other than the women in my family, I couldn't find any heroes. I started to feel a constant sense of erasure when it came to my lived experiences. Brown female voices and experiences were missing from history books, from positions of power, from the boardrooms and on TV screens – except for the infamous Meera Syal and the *Goodness Gracious Me* team. Maybe that's why I became so obsessed with Princess Jasmine when I was little – I had the doll, the lunchbox, the pyjamas, the movie on cassette, the whole shebang! The Middle Eastern representation of her has had scrutiny over the years, and though she wasn't Punjabi, she was *my* princess. But did getting married and being saved by Aladdin have to be my only aspiration? If anything, I found Aladdin more relatable. You see, there wasn't much to work with as a young brown girl . . .

What made being a young brown girl so difficult was the constant messaging that my heritage – who I was and am – was less desirable, fashionable or even legitimate than white Western culture. Eventually, I found myself wanting to deny my own heritage because I was told by society that it had no place here. And with that loss of identity came a lack of self-confidence and self-belief, culminating in me almost losing my entire sense of self. I found myself thinking: where and how do I fit in? I wanted to be white, but I kept thinking 'what am I up against?' Eventually, I had a realization: do I even *need* to fit in?

Brown women are often seen as docile, quiet and passive, thanks to the 'orientalization' of Asian women: dehumanized and reduced. More recently, new stereotypes have been added to our list of labels, including bombers or bashful brides. Isn't it about time that we controlled our narrative and our voice, so that our representation doesn't just consist of the tropes about victimhood and dowries, degradation and despair? Now, this is not me downplaying violence against women or the much-needed ongoing conversations about forced arranged marriages, FGM, grooming and sexual abuse. But the overreliance on a stereotype means that the only facts we have been given about ourselves have been distorted, causing corruption in what we think we know about ourselves. I felt seen and unseen.

How can we define who we are when we've been handed a dictionary full of lies and half-truths? Isn't it up to us to define who the brown woman is or isn't, rather than anyone else?

I didn't want my identity to be defined by how supposedly oppressed I am. Having that as our only label, our only story, just didn't sit right with me. What about the brown women who have changed history? What about our ancestors who fought in anti-colonial movements, and continuing post-independence groups, battling through struggles around war and militarization, against right-wing fundamentalism and state repression? How about the brown women who lived through partition and displacement, the difficulties of migration and assimilation, and, more recently even, through a worldwide pandemic? All whilst trying to untangle prisms of class, caste, community, religion and gender politics. Bloody hell, brown women are strong. This strength reminds us that daring to speak, daring to fight, daring to even exist in a system not designed for you is an act of resistance in itself. Every day, brown women are resisting, challenging and thriving. But where are their stories? Where are the ordinary stories of the daughters and granddaughters, women like us? How about the brown women who inspired me and helped me love who I am, many of whom you'll find in this book?

I'm tired of seeing brown girls typically positioned as 'between two cultures', stuck between Eastern culture and Western culture, and oppressed. I think that picture is just too simplistic. Where are the nuances? What about the brown women who are challenging the status quo? What about being a brown woman with mental health problems? What about being a brown woman and gay? What about being a brown woman and disabled? What about being a brown woman and single? What about being a brown woman in the workplace? Which brown women are already challenging these existing tropes, switching up the narrative but staying connected to their brown identity?

Sometimes I still feel confused about all the layers, dimensions and intersectionality that come with being a young-British-Punjabi-Sikh-Woman-Feminist-Daughter-Wife-Writer-Poet-Teacher, and everything else that comes with those titles. I feel confused by this ongoing metamorphosis, code-switching and people-pleasing. Can you be a brown feminist without rejecting your own culture and fitting into what Western feminist standards dictate? How do you remain true to who you are while trying to navigate a white, male-dominated workspace? Why are brown girls the second-highest performing group of students in the country, yet this isn't reflected in wider institutions? Why, during my years as a teacher, have I seen that brown girls consistently have very low self-confidence and are the least likely to put their hands up in class? Are we the biggest victims of imposter syndrome? How do we manage our daily angst, anger and embarrassment, while balancing it with our happiness, humour and joy? How do we unlearn the messages we have internalized about ourselves? How do we change the conversation in an empowering way? How can we fight back with wisdom, writing and art?

In the advent of fourth-wave feminism, a new era of feminism defined by empowerment, equity, and inclusivity, we've seen brown women in the diaspora starting to find their voice and tell their own story. We're showing we have our place here. And in this fourth feminist wave, I don't want brown women to be left as just a footnote. We need to remind ourselves that we can be feminists without rejecting our culture and identity. The danger of white feminism stems from what can be disguised as allyship in the woman's struggle, actually just putting us down for our 'oppressive cultures and faiths'. Real feminist allies, whatever their colour, take the time to listen to us, our experiences, our truths, from our own voices – not speak for us. Not gaslight. Not pigeonhole.

It's here that I would like to emphasize that identifying as a brown woman can mean a number of things. When I say 'brown women', I mean all women, inclusive of those who identify as such or are gender non-binary. I may use the terms 'brown' and 'South Asian' interchangeably in the book, but I think I prefer brown. But with all these terms, labels, names and phrases, they will change with the context of the time, they will change when the communities those names belong to speak more of their truths. The collections of stories, evidence and themes covered in this book will hopefully reflect some of the realities of those in the diaspora, like the UK, USA, Canada and Australia, that come from 'South Asia'. The heterogeneous, diverse region includes Bangladesh, India, Pakistan and Sri Lanka, but I've tried to be inclusive of those from cross-cutting countries with similar faiths and religions, such as Nepal and Afghanistan. We'll also hear some brown women from other diasporic countries such as Mauritius, Kenya and Uganda. I also recognize and emphasize that this is not one homogenous group. We all have different faiths and beliefs, languages and cultural traditions, interwoven with varying issues of class and caste privilege. But I have tried my best to start unpacking some of the experiences and questions that arise whilst navigating the world in a brown woman's body. Questions like – how can we support and equip brown women with the confidence and tools they need to navigate the difficulties which come with an intersectional identity? I will be exploring key issues such as the home, the media, the workplace, education, mental health, culture, confidence and the body. And we'll see how the digital age has helped these women own their own voices and dictate how their stories are told and how they want to be seen by the world. But we'll dive into that a bit more in Chapter 9.

I recently saw a great image on Instagram by a young Bengali cartoonist called Deya. The picture described the three stages of what she called the 'Diaspora Cultural Journey' that many of us young third- or second-gen brown folk go through in the diaspora. In the first phase of our lives, in early childhood, we love our culture. But as we move into phase two, often in our teenage years, there are times where we deny our culture, our roots, our faith, our families. Then, as we enter into our twenties and thirties, we begin to move into stage three, and start to question who we really are, where we belong, and wonder whether it's too late to learn? In the final part of the cultural journey, we begin to recognize our heritage is actually full of treasures, and one day even hope to pass them on. Hopefully, this book will help with the final part of this trajectory and consciousness-raising, and reassure brown women that they are not alone in thoughts, feelings and anxieties.

I can only hope that this book tells the story of struggle, resilience and, most importantly, achievement. When I was younger, I always wished there was a guidebook on how to deal with growing up brown, female, marginalized and opinionated, but there was no blueprint at the time. So, I've collated stories, advice and support from brown women who have gone before with a clear sense of realism and optimism. The interviews which will help answer some of the questions above will come from brown women who have thrived despite all the odds, from authors to politicians, artists to students, aunties to grandmothers. It is paramount that their stories and life lessons are recorded, noted and passed on, so future brown girls feel armed and equipped to take on the world. By hearing the stories of inspirational brown women from across the UK and the diaspora, my hope is that this book will empower brown women to take the wheel, and help others understand the issues facing brown women.

The future – in this political climate, at least – can feel pretty bleak. There are certain world leaders telling women of colour to 'go back home', and others saying Muslim women wearing burqas 'look like letterboxes'. We're seeing cuts to vital public services. We're seeing the language of white supremacy, Islamophobia and Hindutva becoming predominant in public spaces and online. All these things directly impact brown women. But for all the hate, confusion and loneliness the world might have to offer, you will find an equal amount of solidarity with your brown sisters along the way – from your family, your local community, the digital world and, hopefully, this book.

# CHAPTER 1

# BROWN AND DOWN

## *Rethinking Mental Health*

*eventually, i shut myself down like a computer*

*reboot*

*reboot*

*reboot*

*black screens and flickers*

*sitting inside a haunted house, living with ghosts inside my chest*

*but no one can see them, so no one believed me*

*no one believed me*

*so i had to perform my own invasive surgery*

*open up my chest and remove the disease*

*i saved me*

*now it's time for recovery*

*recovery*

'**A**m I dying?' I thought, as I sat on the bathroom floor, hugging my knees to my chest and clutching on to the sleeves of my hoody. 'Is this a heart attack?' I was only twelve at the time, and this was the closest comparison I could make to what was happening to my body. My heart felt like it was about to burst out of my chest, my body was consumed by cold sweats. I could barely breathe. It felt like a plastic bag had been wrapped around my head, with just enough space to inhale. My lips were salty with tears. Eventually, I sensed my fingertips begin to numb, and I felt paralysed. I later learnt that this was the first of the many panic attacks to come. Many of them took place on bathroom floors and in cubicles like this, behind locked doors where no one could see or hear me. They have all become a bit of a blur, but the worst ones have indelibly tattooed themselves into my memory. Have you ever heard that old saying 'smell is the last memory to go'? Well, I still remember the smell of bleach. Or maybe it wasn't so much the smell, but the number of times I stared at the bottle for a little longer than I should, contemplating . . . Wanting it all to be over.

For years, I never told a soul about anything I was going through. And that's because I had always heard such negative labels given to brown folk suffering from mental health issues. The ongoing stigma forced me to remain closed off, and the fear of being ostracized forced me to silence the suffering caused by my anxiety attacks and depression. I heard that people with depression have bad *karam*, meaning bad karma, and some brown cultures put this down to having made mistakes in a previous life. That meant that the pain and suffering were deserved. I'd also heard that people – or should I say, women – with depression could never get married. No one is gonna accept a crazy brown bride, I was told! I started to believe – and accept – that people with depression or mental health problems bring shame on the family.

With no one to speak to and no outlet for my emotions, I turned to my favourite place for some much-needed comfort – I turned to books. But none of the stories looked like mine or sounded like mine, and that just made me feel even more alone . . . So, at the age of thirteen, I started writing my own story, I started turning the chaos in my mind into something beautiful. I opened up my maroon, leather-bound journal (which I still have!) and started writing down everything I was thinking and feeling, the things I'd experienced in my childhood, the bullying going on at school, how afraid I was of the world. Every time I felt triggered, and all those scary thoughts echoed in my head, I turned to the pen and to poetry. For a long, long time, this was my only form of therapy.

But the loneliness had such a detrimental effect on my self-confidence. I would never put my hand up in class, even though I knew the answers. I was a smart kid and did exceptionally well in all my exams, As and A*s across the board, so outwardly, people always assumed there was nothing wrong with me. I seemed fine, but really that was down to my good ol' friend, high functioning anxiety. Sometimes I wonder if I could have pushed myself more if I hadn't hated myself so much . . .

When I was at university, and after a nasty abusive relationship, I fell into my darkest period of depression, and this was when I remember my self-esteem being at an all-time low. I didn't want to look at myself in the mirror. I couldn't make eye contact with people. I was falling into that abyss that those who have suffered from depression will know all too well. There were days when I wouldn't even leave my bed, let alone my house. So I turned to poetry again – the only thing that made me feel like I had some power inside of me – until I finally decided to seek more help.

Fast forward to a couple of years later in 2017, and there I was, sharing my mental health story on a TEDx stage at the Sadler's Wells Theatre in Angel, in front of 1,200 strangers. I told them how poetry had saved my life. For someone who had been silent for so long this seemed bat shit crazy, I know! But I was so tired of burying so many skeletons inside of me in order to feel alive again, and I knew if poetry and writing helped save me, it could save someone else. In my talk, I questioned why we, in our brown communities, have equated strength with silence. What terrifies me, and what I wanted us to ask, is why is this still the case? Because having anxiety or depression can feel like one of the loneliest feelings in the world. I wonder how many brown girls just like me are sitting on bathroom floors with a never-ending chain of worries catastrophizing in their heads right at this very moment . . .

I appreciate that this might be a heavy chapter to start this book. But I think it's important that we begin from this open, honest and vulnerable place. To allow ourselves to be seen, really seen. Knowing our own darkness in order to find light. And it's from this place of vulnerability that we can start to find courage, to find progress. To find healing.

## *The last taboo*

Before we dive into some of the data and statistics on brown women's mental health – limited as they are – we need to remember to re-emphasize that brown folk are not a homogenous group. So depending on their class, race, gender and sexuality, their mental health experiences will be different. There are different levels of education and wealth which affect brown women in different ways. For some women, the reasons for their mental health issues may relate to bereavement, bullying, neglect, domestic violence and emotional, physical or sexual abuse, while for others, it may be none or all of these things. There are varying states of acceptance across all 'South Asian' groups. There is no single brown mental health experience, but this chapter will try to outline as many of these voices as possible. I'll be looking into a range of mental health areas, such as intergenerational trauma, postnatal depression, eating disorders and, crucially, how we can find ways to heal.

Where do we even start with something that is not meant to exist in our culture? Mental health problems are not meant to hold any space within us, and if they do, we do not admit them out loud. But they do hold space within us, and the more we bottle them up, the more likely they are to explode. We all grew up with stories about that auntie down the road who never got married because she was depressed, or how so-and-so's daughter never leaves the house because she's *pagal*. When I spoke to Poorna Bell, journalist and author of *Chase the Rainbow*, she explained that 'these examples are usually used as the bogeyman of what happens to you when you have a mental illness.' Once that label has been attached to someone, many believe it can never be removed. We've seen and heard words like *izzat* and *sharam* passed down from generation to generation, sometimes with different nuances, but always with the same pain. But it's time that we, as the young generation of brown women, attempt to navigate our wellbeing and change the discourse about our mental health with autonomy, and it's vital that we actively participate in that change.

The existing, and very inadequate data, suggests that the prevalence of common mental disorders such as anxiety and depression is twice as likely in brown women than their white counterparts, at a shocking 63.5 per cent.[1] The same applies to more complex mental health needs. According to Professor Dinesh Bhugra, mental health and diversity specialist at the Institute of Psychiatry at King's College London, 'we know that rates of attempted suicide among South Asian women are two and a half times more than white women, and the 18–24 age group is particularly vulnerable.' Studies have also found that if brown women try to seek treatment, they are often over-prescribed medication such as antidepressants, benzodiazepines, sedatives, antipsychotics, and mood stabilizers. This, alongside several other barriers that we shall unpack later, often stops brown women from accessing the mental health support they might need. But before brown women even arrive at this point in their mental health journey, what's been stopping them from seeking help? Have they been fighting a number of wars already, arising from cultural, familial and religious expectations?

The ingrained acceptance of secrecy has become more and more dangerous. Asian women have been taught to have self-control and restraint when it comes to darker emotions. An outward expression of such feelings is seen as a poor reflection on the individual and her family. A lot of this is attributed to misunderstandings and misconceptions about mental health. There is an association with black magic, bad karma, the will of God or even bad parenting. These stigma-ridden slurs are often combined with intergenerational conflict for brown women, with older generations having their own views on mental health and younger generations having very different interpretations. Alongside wider cultural viewpoints, there are often faith-specific reasons given, which could include Hindu beliefs in karma that suggest an individual's present circumstances are a consequence of past choices and actions. Or within the Muslim community, mental ill health can be attributed to the evil eye, magic, or Jinn possession. Geography also plays a role in this. Because certain cultural groups frequently settle in the same area and the community is tight-knit, there is a fear about news travelling fast. People don't often realize that this ongoing stigma affects us all, from grandmothers with dementia all the way down to granddaughters with anxiety disorders. Regardless of age, each generational group has had to carry the burden of emotional distress as a result.

In Diljeet Bhachu's poem 'Shorts', featured in *The Colour of Madness*, she says, 'talking: my family knows how to talk. We talk a lot. But we don't know how to *talk*.' For a community that loves to talk, we find it hard to ask the hard questions, the real questions. It's about time we started having those awkward dinner table conversations.* We should be able to naturally discuss emotions and mental health around the dinner table

---

* [*awkward dinner table conversations*, noun; conversations that tackle taboo topics and stereotypes in the Asian community]

because they are natural. Often, we're left to make sense of what our mind is doing entirely on our own, and after all that, we're expected to keep quiet and carry on. But this is costing too many lives. I say, no more.

Depression is often seen as a 'white or Western problem'. Even though there are areas of the mental health conversation dominated by whiteness, the associated pain and emotions are obviously not owned by one race. It's often a mistaken belief that most South Asian communities have no direct word for depression or mental health, but some words are seen to be synonymous with it. In Hindi, Urdu and Punjabi you'll find words like *udaas*, to be sad or going through difficulty, or *mansik sayat*. In Gujarati, there is the word *hatasa*, meaning frustration. Bengali and Arabic also have vocabulary very similar to the term depression: *bişannatā* and *kaba*. The importance here isn't so much that there isn't a direct translation with the English language – in fact, there doesn't need to be. Our tongues don't need to mould to a Western vocabulary in order to translate our cultural values or beliefs. Some Western concepts have little value to us. Many Western definitions of wellbeing don't acknowledge the holistic interconnection between physical health, social and family wellbeing and spiritual wellbeing, as many South Asian cultures do.[2] However, our tongues do need to start talking about how we feel. We do need to move away from using the stigmatized terms, like *pagal*, which I've heard being used to describe anything from mania to dementia!

Language is important. Words hold weight and meaning, so it's important we use them wisely within our homes and our families to help us change the narrative around mental health in our communities. This conversation will only get more comfortable with time. Charities such as SOCH Mental Health are directly tackling the conversation taboo within South Asian communities. In Hindi, Urdu and Punjabi, SOCH (ਸੋਚ) means 'to think' or 'a thought'. The charity was set up by two community mental health nurses, Jasmeet Chagger and Maneet Chahal, who passionately believe that the way to combat the stigma surrounding mental health is to change how our communities 'think' about mental health.

## A damaging inheritance

There has been a lot of discussion around the impact that inter-generational trauma may have on the current generation of young brown women. The first conversations around the trans-generational transmission of trauma took place in the 1960s when research began into the impact of Holocaust trauma on children and then grandchildren of survivors. The study found that there was an increased vulnerability to psychological distress and post-traumatic stress disorder (PTSD) even in the second generation.[3] The transmission of this trauma is obviously unintentional, often without awareness of the original traumatic event's contribution. Unlike other inherited conditions, ancestral trauma is not caused by mutations to the genetic code itself. I'm not going to give you a lesson on epigenetics, but what we do need to understand from current scientific research is that events in someone's life can change how their DNA is expressed and that change can, in fact, be passed on to the next generation. That means the genes are modified without changing the DNA code itself.[4]

This theory is yet to be thoroughly analysed for the South

Asian community. Still, considering our very recent history of British colonialism, war, genocide, famine, partition and even natural disasters, combined with government policies on immigration and systemic racism, it is only reasonable to suggest that we, as second and third generations, may be 'holding' some of our parents' and grandparents' pain within us. Often, during traumatic moments in history, it is women who have paid the highest price through gender-specific acts such as trafficking, kidnapping and rape, or what the UN calls 'weapons of war'. When I spoke with Dr Rima Lamba, the Clinical Director and Founder of the Blue River Psychology clinic, she even suggested that 'repeated, interpersonal, relational, and complex traumas can alter our sense of safety when it comes to our bodies, relationships, and the outer world.' She went on to state that 'we pass on our sense of feeling unsafe through how we relate to our children.'

I fully appreciate that our parents and grandparents may never have had the chance to fully heal. All their past pains and difficulties were then interwoven with immigrating to a whole new country and setting a foundation for our existence. This can often lead to parenting from a place of fear, rather than from a place of comfort. When the only priority in parenting is to survive, then how can we thrive? Psychoanalyst and professor M. Gerard Fromm writes that 'what human beings cannot contain of their experience – what has been traumatically overwhelming, unbearable, unthinkable – falls out of social discourse, but very often on to and into the next generation as an affective sensitivity or a chaotic urgency.'[5] Are we now the generation to break the cycle, the never-ending trickle of trauma that has seeped into our bloodlines? Are we now the generation of healing, so that our daughters and our granddaughters will get to live outside of this kind of pain? As things currently stand, there are still no guidelines on how support and treatment can be provided to South Asian women who will be sensitive to all this. That being said, many of the mental health services fall short of culturally sensitive, culturally informed and historically mindful advice. Even if brown women do have some success in accessing services, they're often inappropriate to their needs.

I remember when I eventually sought out counselling during university to combat my ongoing anxiety and depression, I was offloading childhood traumas, my history of being bullied in school and current young adolescent stresses. The therapist, a white woman in her late forties, completely misread all my verbal and non-verbal cues. She suggested I 'move out from home', become more 'independent' and 'stand up' to my family. She was completely unaware of how close-knit Punjabi families are and how their love for me and my love for them was very much a part of my decision-making process. I felt so misunderstood and, if anything, more depressed. I felt both invisible and hypervisible, distorted and unseen. It was unfortunate that my first encounter with a therapist, after being reluctant to find help for so long, was this disappointing and confusing. Over time, I realized how frequently this 'white lens' was applied in therapy. Brown women have found that mental health service providers hold an unconscious bias, automatically viewing Asian cultures as repressive, and therefore assume the treatment of depression was to be found in the adoption of a more Western lifestyle. But this can be even more harmful to the individual, who is made to feel they need to strip parts of their identity. This mistrust towards mainstream mental health services is then further amplified for many minority groups by over-prescribing medication and, for more extreme cases, even involuntary sectioning under the Mental Health Act (1983).

Reflecting on my first therapist's suggestion of 'independence', I often think about how gendered discourses of independence overlay with racialized ones. Studies have shown that service providers see South Asian women as passive and with less autonomy. That's why phrases such as those I heard are also an implicit message to 'leave your oppressive culture', stemming from a lack of understanding of that culture. This, in fact, excludes brown women from a range of provisions such as adequate counselling with a strong client–therapist fit. There's a tendency for brown women to feel they need to put on an act when accessing mental health services, feeling like they need to step closer to whiteness. The inadequacy of mental health services, at all levels, goes hand in hand with broader race inequalities in society. Guilaine Kinouani, a radical psychologist, equality consultant and founder of Race Reflections, has stated that 'psychiatric units look too much like inner cities, poorly designed; chaotic, full of despair and of people of colour with slumped shoulders and vacant gaze. Always, such structures provide a microcosm of violence, inequalities, injustices and abuses of power that exist at macro-level.'[6]

## Fitting the image

Throughout their lives, Asian women are one of the high-risk groups for mental health illnesses, especially for postnatal depression. Brown women with postnatal depression frequently report feeling ashamed when receiving their diagnosis. They feel it will reflect poorly on their abilities as a mother and even more negatively on their family's reputation. Of course, these expectations could apply to all new mums, but brown women face an additional pressure from their in-laws, parents and society to have children immediately after their marriage (the aunties are still on my case!). New mums may then feel that it's a failure to admit that they are struggling, especially to families excited about welcoming a child. Lawyer and business owner Sabrina Kumar suffered from both prenatal and postnatal depression. She told me how this pressure from wider family members 'makes you question your self-worth, understanding and ability to be a "good" mother because every action is questioned.' She went on to say, 'People assume if you look and sound presentable, then you must be fine. It took me two years after my son's birth to realize I was engulfed in postnatal depression and guilt.'

On 27 July 2020, Nima Bhakta, a young mum from California, tragically died by suicide. Nima had been suffering from postnatal depression, and before she died, she wrote, 'It was something you guys wouldn't understand because the Indian society does not fully understand postpartum depression.' Nima's death sent shock waves through social media, triggering the hashtag #BreakTheStigma4Nima. The campaign encouraged South Asian mums across the globe to share their stories and reminded us all that we should not have to suffer in silence. Broader issues like the lack of funding in postnatal care also mean that Asian women face fragmented and irregular support from antenatal care to birth and postnatal, hurried through a system which counted them more as a number than as a person with specific care needs. The whole process can feel gruelling, but as we will see later on in the chapter, it doesn't have to be a lonely one.

It isn't only in motherhood that these issues are exacerbated for brown women through lack of appropriate support, funding and research. The same goes for brown girls suffering from eating disorders, including anorexia, bulimia and binge eating. A YouGov poll commissioned by Beat (formerly Eating Disorders Association) found that nearly 4 in 10 (39%) people believed eating disorders were more common amongst white people than other ethnicities, despite clinical research confirming that eating disorders are just as common or even more common among the brown community. Ballari, who suffers from anorexia and bulimia, told Beat that her mixed-race South Asian ethnicity played a large role in her illness. She said, 'My father spent a lot of time learning you do not need to be a white, privileged teenage girl to have an eating disorder.' Ballari added, 'The harsh reality is eating disorders do not discriminate.' There is a vital lack of education and awareness about eating disorders within the South Asian community as a whole, but what makes this particular issue even more problematic is our unhealthy obsession with thinness and losing weight. This is most likely where many body-image distortions stem from.

I know that food is a massive part of any culture, and brown communities are no different. Any large family gathering is usually accompanied by a big enough spread to feed a small village. But our relationship with food and body image is where the problem lies. We're encouraged to learn how to cook, socialize, and eat – but not too much for women because there will be plenty of auntie eyes watching. The ideal of curvy, full-bodied female figures, which were once a sign of beauty and prosperity in South Asia, has now moved towards a slim figure in the last decade. Combine the auntie pressure* with standard peer pressure, pictures of thin celebrities – Bollywood and Western – splashed across every social media channel and it becomes consistent fat-shaming. You get a toxic mix. The obsession with brown girls needing to be 'slim and trim', in the words of Sima Taparia from the Netflix series *Indian Matchmaking*, can prime individuals to develop disordered eating habits and behaviours. There may even be pressure from partners and husbands.

For a long time, mostly when my depression was at its worst, I had a really unhealthy relationship with my body. I would associate thinness with eating less, and at times where I felt I had no autonomy in my life, I thought that food was the only thing I could control. Like almost all young women, whatever their race or colour, when I was complimented on my thinness, I accepted it as validation. I had to ignore other people's opinions, especially from the aunties . . . 'Boys like thin girls', I would hear, as I went for a second helping of barfi. What this tells young women is that their bodies are solely made for the pleasure and desire of men. Well, forget that. I wanted to have my slice of cake and eat it too. I started training in kickboxing over six years ago, and rather than focusing on losing weight, I focused on making my body and mind feel stronger. It took many years to unlearn the toxic behaviour reinforced by the media, by aunties and by

* [*auntie pressure*, noun; the unsolicited advice given by older female members of the Asian community, usually concerning weight, skin colour and relationships]

myself. I had to form a new relationship with my body, one that was focused on self-care, acceptance and health, rather than size. And definitely not based on what a man wants.

There has been so much conversation about the self-worth and wellbeing of women as a whole, which does not take into account how particularly destructive patriarchy can be for brown women. The ongoing expectations are particularly strong for brown women to focus their entire life's worth on being a tripartite woman – a mother, a wife and daughter-in-law. Even without the threat of mental health issues, this pressure can be exhausting. The expectation and need to people-please and sacrifice our own desires seems particularly inherent in our culture.

This is something Poorna noted when I spoke to her. 'We seem to be pleasing other people to the detriment of our own mental health, whether that's the amount of stress that you're under, the obligations that you're taking on or the amount of sleep that you're sacrificing. This idea, specifically as South Asian women, that you have to sacrifice everything for the betterment and comfort of other people is something that is drummed into us from a very young age. It's not all bad, because I understand that doing things for your community, friends and family is a noble effort, but all too often we are told to do this at great sacrifice to ourselves, and we're never taught that we need to be looking after ourselves and making sure we're OK before we take care of other people.'

## Patriarchy punishes us all

Fathers, husbands, brothers, sons – all men have a role to play here too. Research conducted by Time to Change, a charity that I'm proudly an ambassador for, also highlighted the role that men play in either allowing or restricting access to formal support for women with mental health problems. This dependence on male support can leave many women, already hindered by the community's social norms around mental health problems, even more isolated and without the means to recover.[7]

But what I wish I could show the world is that this type of toxic masculinity and patriarchy isn't just impacting brown women but also impacting brown men too. These attitudes are the same motivators that encourage brown men to be raised as stoic and strong. It's the same reason men are told not to express their emotions and not to cry. I believe the 'golden child' syndrome also has a role to play here. Because of the ongoing preference for sons in our community, boys are often put on a pedestal and, as we know, get spoilt rotten. While on the other hand, brown girls are seen and openly talked about as a burden, and we'll explore how damaging this is to a young girl's self-worth in Chapter 8. For brown boys, what also comes with this pedestal is the duty to carry on the family name and take responsibility for looking after the family later on in life. Soon there are bills to pay, mouths to feed and shoes to fill. And we know this can be tough. Maybe this gets stressful? Maybe they feel ill-equipped? Maybe they just need a shoulder to cry on? But we have told boys throughout their lives that those tears are out of place.

I've seen personally how this forces men to stay bottled up, and rather than being able to express their emotions in healthy ways, prompts them to turn to other outlets such as drugs, alcohol and other forms of addiction. For some men, the burden might be too much to bear. The statistics are harrowing, with men making up 75 per cent of suicides in the UK. In fact, suicide is still the single biggest killer of men under the age of forty-five.[8] I have even heard families describing the loss of male family members to suicide as a 'brain attack' because they were so reluctant to discuss the reality of the mental health struggles they may have faced. So, if this culture of toxic masculinity, patriarchy and stigma is destroying both brown men and women in our communities, why the hell are we allowing it to continue?

Another aspect that can't be ignored within this conversation around mental health is how, even now, non-heterosexual relationships and gender non-conformity have been pathologized by the brown community. The irony here is that South Asia has a long history of accepting non-heterosexual relationships, gender non-binaries and of exploring sexuality. It was Section 377 of the Indian Penal Code that criminalized homosexuality as a result of British colonial law. Thankfully it was revoked in 2018. In 1871, the British also criminalized hijras, who were widely accepted amongst brown folk. Since 2014, hijras have been officially and legally recognized as a third gender. But still, we know that there are significant barriers stopping our LGBTQ+ community speaking openly about their real mental health needs. Imagine feeling like a minority within a minority. As Priyanka Meenakshi, writer and artist for *Gal-Dem* and *Consented*, shared in the *Colour of Madness*, 'as a brown gender non-conforming lesbian under capitalism, simply living in the world is violent'. One of the leading voices in this space is my good friend, Sanah Ahsan. Sanah is a queer, Muslim Pakistani woman, who recently qualified as a clinical psychologist. She was also a reporter for Channel 4's *Young, British and Depressed*. Sanah describes how she felt that she grew up with 'internalized messages shoved down my throat . . . Too queer to be Muslim, and too Muslim to be queer', that led her to a near-fatal overdose over ten years ago. Thankfully, Sanah is now healthy and thriving and is currently working on her thesis on whiteness in clinical psychology and higher education. She is using her platform to make sure brown queer voices are not ignored in the mental health conversation.

## *Keeping it in the family*

During the time of writing this book, I became a carer for my grandma-in-law, and it made me realize that with a rapidly growing South Asian elderly population, soon there will be an increasing concern for both carers and those in need of care. According to data from World Population Prospect, by 2050, 1 in 6 people in the world will be over sixty-five.[9] Caring for a person with chronic illness or mental health needs exerts a huge psychological, physical and emotional toll. And I've seen firsthand how hard it is to do alone. As the old saying goes, it can take a village. It can also be a very isolating experience. Artist and producer Dawinder Bansal became a young carer at the age of eleven when her mum was diagnosed with a mental illness. Dawinder told me how 'being a carer is a serious business. It is paying full and proper attention to their habits, changes in behaviour, new ailments . . . It's about being responsible for the mental and physical wellbeing, and often, the wellbeing of a carer is not last on the list. It's simply not even on the list.'

30

It's pretty common within brown families for an individual to look after an unwell family member on their own, viewing care as less of a necessity and more as an opportunity to reciprocate familial support. Dawinder said, 'As someone who has been a carer for thirty years, I don't regret caring for my mother. Not one bit. It is an honour and a blessing to look after my loving and kind mother who gave me life.' Although this is great and much to be applauded, much of this responsibility inevitably falls on the brown woman. BBC broadcaster and producer Amrit Matharu also became a carer for her grandparents at a young age. She tells me: 'Caring can be a heavy responsibility, but as a child, I didn't realize it was like that. They were just things I felt I was expected to do as a good daughter or granddaughter – this is quite a common thing I felt in an Asian household. I have very vivid memories of taking my grandparents to the doctors and acting as their translator. I do have some fun memories of this, though, like when my grandma misinterpreted a doctor's question about "alcohol" as fizzy drinks! It was the running joke in the family for a while.'

A stigma still exists for the carer who might want to look at palliative care for their relative. This stigma often causes the carer to be reluctant to ask for help for the individual's mental health needs and their own. But we shouldn't be ashamed or afraid to ask for help. Manisha Tailor MBE is a former primary school teacher turned entrepreneur, who launched a company that uses football and education to help those with mental health problems integrate within our society. At the age of eighteen, her twin was diagnosed with schizophrenia and sectioned under the Mental Health Act (1983), as a consequence of long-term torment and bullying, resulting in Manisha becoming a young carer. She told me: 'In the early years of my brother's condition, as a family, we had many smirks and the turning of noses from those in our community, including relatives. It was a challenging time – people just did not understand how to act or behave when they saw my brother.' She went on to explain how her brother's condition and her role as a carer required her family to 'build resilience in the face of others . . . It was horrible for my mum to hear comments such as "who will want to marry your daughter now?"' Sadly, brown folk still love to label and shun entire families in situations like this. But this hasn't stopped Manisha. Her advocacy work through football has been a creative way of breaking the stigma and highlighting carers and their families' needs.

However, there is still a lot more work to be done to make sure that we are supporting the mental health needs of both the carer and the individual requiring care. Since understanding the effects that caring has had on her mental and physical health, Amrit tells me how important it was to stay aware of what her body and mind were telling her. 'I realized that if I wasn't looking after myself, I couldn't look after others. So, taking time out for myself became so important. It can be easy to forget when you have so much going on and people to look after, so I am still learning how to do this [. . .] More importantly I began talking about what is happening in my personal life to friends and at times with my workplace. Sometimes you can feel embarrassed or shy to tell people what you're dealing with, but I realized that they can't help you as they will think everything is fine if they don't know. Since doing this, I've had a lot of support, and it's actually really comforting having people send you kind messages and knowing others care for you too.'

## *A seismic shift*

With all these overlapping aspects within the mental health conversation and so many areas to improve for brown women, the mission might seem overwhelming. Impossible even. I felt this way for a long time: disheartened, alone and with no sign of light at the end of the tunnel. Yet I think there is a shift happening, a really big shift that will change how we speak about mental health in our homes, our communities, and, most importantly, in our own heads. And it's important that we all take part in the movement.

One of the first steps needs to be towards a communal sense of healing. Healing will only come about properly when influenced by a collective community discourse. We cannot do this alone. For me, this collective sense of healing had to start at home, something I'd been putting off for years . . . One day, on an average Monday afternoon in 2017, as I sat there marking some GCSE practice papers just before heading out to a poetry gig, I saw an email pop up in my inbox. I'd been invited to do a TED talk on how I'd been using creative expression and writing to support my mental health journey. I thought it was amazing that only after a year of performing and sharing my work online did I get these incredible requests. So I took the 'say yes and figure out the rest later' approach, and I began the painstaking yet healing task of writing my talk, entitled 'How Poetry Saved My Life'. But I realized that if I was really going to deliver this talk to my biggest audience yet, and with its potential to reach TED's global audience, it was about time that I spoke to my parents about my anxiety for the very first time. It was the first of many conversations my family and I had about mental health, and I instantly felt such a weight had been lifted. They, of course, had a lot of questions. But there were no stigma-ridden slurs, no judgement – just a sense of healing ... My mum suffers from serious claustrophobia. When I explained to her that this was actually a type of anxiety disorder and that my anxiety attacks feel very similar, she found it easier to empathize. I had a very similar conversation with my mother-in-law after I got married. I wanted to start our relationship from an honest place. So we had a frank discussion about anxiety, my triggers, and what support I needed during my low days. Poorna tells me she's also been able to have more of these open and frank conversations with her parents. 'Rather than things coming out a few months down the line, or in some cases a few years down the line (which is what makes a lot of families dysfunctional), it means we're dealing with our baggage as and when it unfolds. It's not always perfect, but it allows us to communicate what we need from each other.'

Through all of these very tough conversations, I'm adamant that a change in our language as a community could lead to a huge shift in our current generation, which could result in healthier and more holistic outcomes for brown women and, by extension, the whole community. So, for example, projects like Taraki, founded by Shuranjeet Singh, are working with Punjabi communities to reshape mental health approaches. Taraki, a verb found in Urdu, Punjabi and Hindi, means 'to progress' – to develop, to move towards an improved or more developed state. One of their mission statements is to co-develop and implement 'projects which improve mental health awareness within Punjabi communities through dialogue and community engagement'. Hopefully, this community-led approach could lead to more participatory research to gather the data behind our mental health needs. The community discourse and data can then be used within mental health awareness campaigning to include the brown voice. For example, helping to inform awareness-raising campaigns by targeting them with the information needs of specific groups, or tailoring them in a way that is culturally sensitive.[10]

As Poorna beautifully put it, 'By talking, we can create a space for people going through something similar, to reach out before it's too late . . . That is the spirit of community and a key path to prevention.'

These types of community spaces will make a significant impact on healing our intergenerational trauma too. Through talking, through sharing and through learning, we can slowly unpack all the baggage we have been carrying with us for decades. In his book *It Didn't Start with You* (such a fitting title!), Mark Wolynn discusses how inherited family trauma shapes who we are and how breaking the cycle requires tuning into and giving space to those ancestral stories in order to heal. This is why education about our history and identity, not only in schools but also in our homes and communities, can go a long way. Understanding our history is key to unlocking our healing.

This learning and unlearning would also have an additional benefit. There's been research since the 1980s into how a sense of strong identity can have a beneficial impact on our mental wellbeing and self-worth. By understanding our recent histories, especially those of our parents and grandparents, we will develop a stronger sense of who we are, we'll feel a sense of uniqueness, competency and more in control of our narrative.[11]

Community spaces, both online and face-to-face, could be the perfect place to explore this. We know that there are many areas to repair within the South Asian diaspora, but we are the generation that are starting to heal. By learning and understanding our recent histories, we are doing the inner work needed. Perhaps we'll even be able to release our children from lugging these traumas with them into their future. Perhaps we can liberate them from the generational chain.

Satveer Nijjar, a winner of Most Inspirational Person of the Year MBCC 2018 and founder of Attention Seekers, an accredited self-harm awareness course, recognizes the need to discuss difficult mental health topics in the broader community. Satveer delivers workshops to school-based staff and students, housing staff, doctors, nurses and social workers, but has also begun providing courses in places of worship. 'I have been fortunate enough to have delivered in a number of Gurdwaras, delivering sessions on self-harm awareness to the *sangat* [community] in both English and Punjabi . . . I found that members of the *sangat* were grateful to have someone speak about topics that they felt were taboo. I remember a woman coming to speak to me in the toilets after my presentation, she was in tears saying that she related to so much of my story and wished she could have spoken up earlier. These experiences have given me hope for future generations.'

This community work and research can then feed into one of the biggest fights – urging mental health services to think beyond a white, Eurocentric model of counselling and therapy. When I spoke to Aisha Sheikh-Anene, the chair of the Board of Trustees at the Mental Health Foundation, she told me that one of her main concerns for brown women's mental health is the 'unmet need for culturally sensitive counselling and therapy'. Whether it's called cultural humility, cultural competence, or cultural effectiveness doesn't really matter; what matters is that we have seen what the absence of it feels like. I'm here to tell you it feels pretty shit, and it can result in inappropriate or unhelpful advice being given to young brown women like me who need support. What we need is empathy. What we need is curiosity without being patronized. What we need is respect. What we need is the recognition that our mental distress might be expressed and experienced differently from our white counterparts.[12] All of these things come with a heightened understanding and appreciation of the social context of the patient, and actually listening to and learning from the voices of brown women.

That's why Raj Khaira set up *South Asian Therapists*, a global directory of South Asian therapists. The website has an incredible search engine that allows you to search for a therapist by geographical region and by what kind of session would suit you best, be it online, in person, over the phone or even a home visit. A one-stop shop for a brown therapist or counsellor that best suits you. It's brilliant! I actually found my most recent therapist through the directory, and wow, has she changed my life. We've recently been observing my decisions made out of fear, obligation and guilt (F.O.G.), an issue that's very common amongst brown women, and my overall people-pleaser problems, but we'll come back to that later in the book. *South Asian Therapists* directory helped me find a therapist with cultural competence, which was miles different to my disastrous first encounter with a therapist. However, we still need to see existing public and community service providers urgently improving their cultural competence too. This is incredibly important for young brown women, or even older brown women, who don't have the financial means to seek help privately and pay for therapy.

## *Doing it for the kids*

For the mental health of young brown kids, schools and teachers inevitably have a role to play here, and I've personally seen how teacher support could go a long way. If you are a teacher, model good habits like talking about mental health openly and healthily. If a pupil shares their worries with you, give them the time and a safe space to talk, don't try to 'fix' their problem or immediately refer them on to another member of staff or service. Empathy involves attempting to understand things from their perspective, and avoiding judgement. If you have any concerns about their safety, follow your school's safeguarding policy and discuss the matter with your designated safeguarding lead. Brown kids often feel an almost excessive pressure to do well academically, and as a result they are less likely to participate in extra-curricular activities, which can be another reason for a lack of confidence and low self-esteem, as they may not have the opportunity to find other passions and interests which, in turn, could improve their mental health.

Sport, whether in or out of school, has been proven to play a big role within this. Plenty of research has shown how sports and exercise stimulate chemicals in your brain, including serotonin and endorphins, improving your mood and making you feel good. Manisha saw this first-hand through her work at Wingate & Finchley FC Disabled Fans Forum and how it helped people like her brother when he was diagnosed with schizophrenia. 'Football can play a vital role in empowering those with mental illness to channel their thoughts and feelings into something positive. Football truly has the power to change lives and provide those with mental illness with a sense of belonging.' She went on to describe how these spaces offer 'a safe environment that fosters confidence, motivation and the feeling of self-worth'. Another brown woman who has used sport to support her mental health journey is the inspirational Anoushé Husain. Anoushé is a disabled para-climber. She was born missing her right arm below her elbow. She's also a cancer survivor and credits para-climbing with completely changing her life. Anoushé told me that 'the wall is a vertical puzzle, and requires me to focus. It's an active meditation, it's mindfulness. It's just you, breathing on the wall, there is no judgement. The wall cannot judge you. You're left with you, with yourself, and it's one of the most freeing feelings.' She said that schools could be doing more to encourage these alternative sports as an option for brown girls. That's why she's a patron for Grit & Rock, a charity which aims to help girls aged thirteen to fifteen from deprived, inner-city areas to develop their self-confidence through a year-long mountaineering training programme.

Speaking of schools, during my days as a secondary school teacher in London, we would often use a teaching method called 'think, pair, share'. Essentially this means a problem is posed to the students, they have time to *think* about it individually, then work in *pairs* to solve the problem and finally *share* their ideas with the class. Not only does this provide positive changes in the students' self-esteem, but their learning is enhanced when they have the opportunity to elaborate their ideas through dialogue. It also allows the students to take ownership of their thoughts as well as understanding others. I have found that it is one of the most effective teaching tools, so why don't we do it in real life? Why don't we 'think, pair, share' more? Imagine if we tried these techniques in our homes, with our friends and family or within our local communities, perhaps these mental health taboos would be a thing of the past.

As well as schools, our workplace institutions have an essential role to play in keeping their workers happy and healthy and providing psychological safety. Workplace microaggressions (which I'll be covering in more detail in Chapter 3) can have a lasting impact on your mental health. This is part of a wider conversation that obviously affects everyone at work, but if you are an employee, do have a look into your workplace's policy on mental health. Do they even have a mental health policy? This will give an indication as to what the workplace culture on mental health is like. It might also be worthwhile looking into the diversity of the workplace itself.

### Find what helps you heal

But before we can make these outward macro changes, is there importance in first turning inwards? Shouldn't we first give ourselves permission to say we are hurting, centre our own psychological needs, and also find those small wins that can help us improve our mental fitness alongside formal mental health support. Things we can start doing on a daily basis? The little things that can make the bigger things feel lighter. For me, it was in poetry. With all its verses and rhymes, with all its grit and grime, with all the air it gave me. Poetry saved my life, time and time again. By writing my pain into existence, turning all that chaos in my mind into something beautiful on a page was my only outlet for a long time. I now have a collection of hundreds of poems, from the very first anxiety attacks as a teenager to my road to recovery in my early twenties. According to research by the All-Party Parliamentary Group (APPG) on arts, health and wellbeing, referring patients to art and poetry would not only alleviate anxiety, depression and stress whilst increasing resilience and wellbeing, it could also save the NHS £216 per patient.[13] Of course it doesn't have to be poetry. It could be dance, singing, playing an instrument, cooking, gardening, writing short stories, digital art or the performing arts. It doesn't even have to be creative and it certainly doesn't have to be expensive. There are so many small ideas that start in a bedroom and maybe, like me, end up one day on a stage, in front of thousands of people. But that doesn't have to be the result, it could be that special thing you keep for yourself or share with a small community of those with similar outlets. It could be journalling, one of the new hallmarks of the wellbeing movement, and all for good reason. Studies have shown that journaling can improve sleep, make your immune system stronger and even boost your I.Q.[14] All those negative emotions built up inside you will have a chance to move around, express themselves and perhaps even come out of you and land on a page.

In George Orwell's *Why I Write* he suggested that there are four key reasons people decide to write. His suggestions were sheer egoism, aesthetic enthusiasm, historical impulse and political purpose. But I would like to add a fifth reason to Orwell's theory. I feel that writing can be used to save ourselves, to heal ourselves and, by doing so and sharing our stories, heal others too. In the words of Anne Frank, 'I can shake off everything as

I write; my sorrows disappear, my courage is reborn.' Writing can be a healer at any age – as soon as you write your thoughts down, you literally feel them leaving your body. Other people may not. But I've seen first-hand in the writing workshops I have facilitated specifically for brown women how they find themselves going through a transformative and expansive process, authoring their truth through their own voice. Hopefully, through this sense of re-authoring, you'll find yourself being a little kinder to yourself too.

You're probably thinking this all sounds quite spiritual, and it is. The journey to heal and recover is most definitely a spiritual one, and there might be methods that are closer to home and support a holistic form of self-healing. Ayurveda, yoga, mindfulness and meditation have been used by brown women since the Vedic century (*c.*1500 – *c.*500 BCE), way before Sweaty Betty started charging over £50 for a yoga mat. We all know how yoga and even meditation have been distorted, capitalized, decontextualized and, in some cases, sexualized in the West, but we'll save that for Chapter 6. Before all that mess, brown women had been practising these disciplines for thousands of centuries. They genuinely have stood the test of time, so lean into them. It's another chance for us to reclaim and relearn our history and heritage, which often gets lost in its Western translation.

Lots of brown women also feel that having a connection with faith can be a profound support to good mental health. It might not be for everyone, but for many brown women, their relationship with their wellbeing is more than secular. South Asian mental health narratives have often portrayed religion as oppressive towards brown women and their wellbeing, but we know this can't always be the case. That singular narrative can't be true for everyone. As a Sikh, I've implemented prayer and meditation into my daily routine. Many Sikhs find the *Sukhmani Sahib* prayer particularly helpful. It literally means 'consoler of the mind' or 'song of peace', signifying the calming effect it has on the mind of the listener or reader. The *Pavamana Mantra* is the name of a Hindu mantra considered valuable for spiritual awakening. It is written in Sanskrit, and can be translated as: 'Om, from falsehood lead me to truth, From darkness lead me to the light, From death lead me to immortality, Om peace, peace, peace.' In Islam, the Prophet Muhammad once said that in prayer, he would find rest and relief (*Nasai*), and there are many *duas* (a prayer of invocation) in the Quran and Sunnah which deal with alleviating feelings of depression, worry and anxiety. Faith shouldn't be used as the catch-all for mental health problems; you should still be getting the formal support services you need. Ultimately, it's all a matter of finding the right equipment for your mental health toolkit.

Recognizing all these particular vulnerabilities within our society will be a revolutionary moment, I am sure of it. I feel the waves coming. We are a society that has been conditioned to bottle ourselves up, but hopefully we are starting to see that it's OK to be vulnerable and, actually, owning that can make us more powerful. And other powerful brown women are giving out the same message. Nadiya Hussain, author, chef and winner of *The Great British Bake Off*, made headlines in 2019 for her openness about her post-traumatic stress disorder and panic attacks. Her raw and honest therapy sessions made it to the main screen in the BBC's documentary *Nadiya: Anxiety and Me*. The documentary received critical acclaim, clocking up four- and five-star reviews across the board. But more importantly, comments came flooding in online after the show, praising Nadiya and calling her an 'example to everyone' . . . 'such a role model for speaking out about her battle with anxiety'. I cried bucketloads watching the documentary; her words felt like my own. Her pain felt like my pain. I can only imagine all the brown women who watched that documentary, seeing a woman who looked like them and sounded like them, reminding them they are not alone in this.

When I spoke to Satveer about her self-harm awareness classes in schools, she said that when telling the students about her own history of self-harm 'one thing that they all had in common was thanking me for my perceived "bravery" in standing up and sharing my own experiences. Many have said they could relate to aspects of my personal story'. Radio and television presenter Anita Rani opened up about her miscarriage in a heartfelt article for *Red* magazine. She wrote: 'I had a miscarriage and it showed me it's okay to be vulnerable [. . .] Don't let the misplaced shame stop you or the fact that it can be very hard to talk about it [. . .] Find someone you trust and tell them. It helps. I hope the piece I've written helps a few of you too.' Through those simple words, through sharing such vulnerability, we have shattered a piece of the wall of stigma. And we shall keep shattering it, by sharing our stories.

Sometimes I still have to remind myself, 'You're not alone in this anymore.' There are still dark days when my anxiety and depression decide to creep back out of the little cave they sit in in my head, scratching to get to the surface. There are days where my chains of worries still threaten to spiral out of control. On those days, I let my loved ones know that I'm 'feeling fragile', and might need some time, patience or extra comfort. That's when I remind myself that being vulnerable does not make me weak. Vulnerability can become strength, and as we've seen, vulnerability can help build connection.

What's really important is that I no longer bottle it up. I can write. I can speak to the people I love. I can use the methods that I learnt in cognitive behavioural therapy with an awesome and understanding therapist. And I now have a community that reminds me that I am worthy. I am soft but strong. I am power-ful. It's important to embrace the strength in vulnerability, the power of community, its networks and local and even ancient knowledge. This is where many brown communities can really come into their own because community is something we have never lost. There is a sisterhood here for you on your road to recovery and mental health management. We'll keep fighting for appropriately funded and culturally sensitive mental health ser-vices. No more stigma-ridden slurs or lazy assumptions. No more silence. Those lonely bathroom floors won't be your only safe space anymore.

# CHAPTER 2

# BEYOND THE CLASSROOM

## *Asian Girls and Education*

*i will always be awkward dinner table conversations*
*i will always be the debater*
*if i learnt anything from j.d.salinger*
*it was to always be the challenger*
*don't be afraid to play the devil's advocate*
*for those that made my gender feel inadequate*
*i will no longer be left on mute*
*quiet and cute*
*this is not what you wanted*
*you wanted a one-word answer*
*but my friend*
*i am not a one-word woman*
*this is for all the times i never put my hand up in class*
*even though i knew the answer*
*even though i knew how to articulate it*
*and debate it*
*but soon i learnt*
*you may be the smartest in the room*
*but maybe that room doesn't let you bloom*
*they kept us quiet so we would never know*
*everyone was killing our confidence so we could never grow*

**smartest in the room**

When I left school and started to navigate the world of university, I began to recognize some clear disparities between myself and the rest of the students. My position. My otherness. My difference. My unspoken alienation. What highlighted these was a conversation I once overheard whilst standing outside one of my seminar rooms. At university, I was that eager student who always arrived on time; in fact, I was the one that always arrived *early*. The goody-two-shoes. Maybe this was my way of fulfilling the model minority stereotype society expected of me – be on time, work twice as hard, don't take your education for granted. That day, I stood outside the seminar room, reading the book I had been enjoying on my daily commute on the tube. I folded the corner of the page and returned the book to my bag as I realized the previous class was leaving the room.

The last to leave was a young brown girl. I'd seen her around during freshers' week earlier that year. She gave me a small smile and left the door slightly ajar. I picked up my bag and was about to head into the room when I heard . . . '*they* are going to be married off as soon as they leave here, so what is the point of raising their expectations?' I stepped back, and felt a huge lump rise in my throat. Did he mean *us*? Us *brown girls*? I walked into the room, and both the lecturer and the teaching assistant looked at me sheepishly. I smiled and said hello politely, as I always did. I sat down, while a million thoughts charged through my head. Did I just smile at them, despite what I just heard? What is wrong with me?

Throughout the rest of the class, I stared blankly at my note-pad, questioning myself. Questioning whether I should really be there. Do I deserve to be there? Was I just a 'token'? Do I tell someone about this? I then started questioning my questions. Why am I making this more difficult? If I was white, would I have to question any of these things? My position here would be normal. I would pat myself on the back and say, 'Well done, Jaspreet, you deserve to be here, you deserve to have high as-pirations and high expectations.' In that moment, I realized I had a bitter pill to swallow: meritocracy is a myth.

I remember going home that day feeling so exhausted. It would be one of the first of many days dealing with this kind of exhaustion. The kind that sits at the top of the spine, leaving tension in your neck. The type of exhaustion that feels like the weight of the world is on your back and makes the pit of your belly ache. The exhaustion that comes from having to constantly navigate the white gaze, the exhaustion of being automatically deemed passive and of entering rooms where we'll never be directly addressed, the exhaustion of always having to work twice as hard, the exhaustion of always having to be on time, or in my case early. All because I was a brown girl. And for what? Was it really, as those lecturers so dismissively pointed out, a complete waste of time? Because surely I was just going to get married and have kids anyway. This exhaustion still lives within us now. It's probably why 'I'm tired' is my new favourite phrase to use in Twitter debates these days.

South Asian girls are actually some of the smartest students in the country. Fact. At every academic level, they follow closely behind Chinese boys and girls in terms of academic achievement. Yet despite this, during my years as a teacher, I have found that Asian girls are the least likely to put their hand up in class. They are the least likely to get involved in class debates or put themselves forward for prestigious school roles. This despite the fact that 53 per cent of Asian girls achieved an average 'Attainment 8' (equivalent to an A*) across their GCSEs, which is way above the national average.[1]

Beyond the classroom, later in life, even though an increasing number of brown women have college or university-level qualifications, South Asian women, especially Bangladeshi and Pakistani Muslim women, remain among the most excluded and lowest paid sections of the labour force.[2] I'm sure many of you have already heard the oft-quoted statistic that there are more FTSE 100 CEOs named Steve and David than there are women and ethnic minority leaders combined.[3] And more widely, data from the Office for National Statistics' Labour Force Survey suggests that Muslim women are up to 65 per cent less likely to be employed than white Christian women of the same age and qualifications. How can any of this make sense? It's clearly not because brown women are not hard-working. Our accolades prove that. So why is that not translating into opportunities, later on in life? It is, of course, because of the wider oppressive structures at play. Structures to do with our gender, ethnicity and perhaps even our class. Unfortunately, it's structural racism and sexism at its very clearest. So where does this all start? And more importantly, what do we do about it? How can we take some of this power back and empower ourselves?

Even now, brown girls are having to live in a society where it's OK for world leaders to have written articles describing the burqa as 'oppressive and ridiculous', comparing Muslim women to 'bank robbers' and 'letterboxes'. We live in a world where the brown girl is consistently being ignored by every establishment, whether it's schools, universities, the workplace, the media or the government. Or rather, we aren't being completely *ignored*. These institutions have played a key role in the construction of our identities. The state and media's interest, or should I say obsession, with young brown girls has only ever reinforced negative stereotypes. Characterizing our cultures and traditions as oppressive, and associating us only with forced marriages, 'honour' crimes, FGM and grooming – these so-called brown girl problems that we need 'saving' from. Of course, I am not belittling the importance of tackling gender-based violence. But I am wondering why these very institutions have not been asking 'what should we be doing better for brown girls?' 'How can we make them feel valued and safe?' 'Are we listening to their needs?' Because they are clearly not doing enough. Our achievements, our aspirations, our very value as human beings, and even our safety all seem to be put at the bottom of the list.

## Sad stereotypes

Within schools, brown girls are seen as hard-working, but teachers ultimately tend to characterize them as quiet and passive, beliefs that stem from outdated historical assumptions about Asian cultures. This perception is reinforced by the racist stereotypes often associated with black pupils who, in contrast to Asian boys and girls, are seen as loud and disruptive. Horrible labels, I know. There has been evidence in the past to show that some teachers assume that brown parents have low aspirations for their daughters' education compared to their sons' because they are more likely to get married earlier.[4] There are also assumptions that their lack of 'freedom' has bred them to be submissive. Even though Asian girls and Chinese pupils might be doing well academically, ultimately they are seen as the 'wrong kind of learner',[5] too quiet and not confident or assertive enough. These stereotypes are in danger of becoming self-fulfilling prophecies if they are not challenged. These attitudes and perceptions, which have a very Eurocentric understanding of culture, fail to recognize the other power struggles at play and downplay the role of race, class and gender constructs that is often at the heart of the persistent struggles of marginalized groups.

When I spoke about these loaded perceptions, Shalina Patel, head of Teaching and Learning in a large comprehensive second-ary school in north-west London, told me how she's seen first-hand how this can play out in the classroom. Shalina is also a history teacher and is one of the founders of The History Cor-ridor on Instagram, a popular page for inclusive history education. She told me that 'This assumed passivity may mean that brown girls are sometimes asked to sit next to more disruptive pupils, with teachers assuming that they are likely to just accept this rather than push back. What impact does that have on them? It's certainly something I have raised as a reflection for teachers to consider when it comes to making seating plans.'

What is clear is that there is a shocking lack of ambition for brown girls. Joyti Kaur, assistant educational psychologist at the University of Leeds, experienced the risks that come with these culturally loaded perceptions first-hand: 'I was told during my A levels that I wouldn't be allowed to apply to certain universities.'

Joyti grew up in Leeds, in one of the most deprived areas of the country. 'Because of the area we lived in, our school had a scheme to encourage students to get into Russell Group universities for fairer access. That application needed to be supported by the school, but my head of year refused to support the application. They said even if I got in, I wouldn't be able to handle the workload.' Joyti says, 'It was only the constant empowerment from my parents that gave me the confidence to do well.'

## Finding our cultural capital

When I taught A-level sociology, I introduced my students to the theories of Pierre Bourdieu, a French sociologist. Much of the class was made up of brown girls, and I could see the look on their faces when they slowly applied Bourdieu's theory of cultural and social capital to their own lives, just as I did when I studied sociology at their age. We explored how these forms of capital refer to someone's tastes, mannerisms, clothing, style of speech and friendship networks, and how they are things that we acquire by being a part of a particular social class. They came up with their own examples to apply to the theory, including knowing someone who can get you a good job or how to conduct yourself in an interview. I could see on their faces that they were questioning whether or not they personally had this kind of cultural and social capital. Some of the girls stuck around after the lesson to have a chat with me. My classroom had become a safe space for them, even outside lessons. It was usually an opportunity for them to vent their frustrations, some of which I knew all too well. Maybe that's why I would consciously spend more time helping these students out. I'd help them with their UCAS applications, writing personal statements and even held mock interviews to prepare them for university interviews. But more importantly, I gave them the time and space to explore their dreams and aspirations for the future. I also used this as a way to challenge them, to get them to see that these notions of cultural capital are a top-down view of parental influence and exclude young people as active agents in shaping their outcomes. I don't know if it was right or wrong for me to give them the extra help, but I wanted them to be on a level playing field with their white counterparts, who I could see were getting work experience placements at investment banks, media outlets and big corporate firms.

This is definitely an area schools and educators could be focusing on more generally, and it would be particularly helpful for brown girls. Tracking students' CVs, looking at their additional experiences, beyond academic grades, in a meaningful and individualized way. It will also show brown girls that they already encompass many skills they should be proud of, like being multilingual, having a diverse worldview, and knowing how to manage multiple stakeholders, from family and friends to school. This process could encourage some capable yet less confident girls to apply for opportunities and positions of responsibility that might broaden their skill sets. Having someone championing you and guiding you can make a world of difference. That's why role models and mentors are so important, and having one that understands your cultural context is best of all. Someone who can stop you from feeling the pressure to conform to prescribed ideals. Dr Sheila Kanani knows this all too well. Sheila is the Education, Outreach and Diversity Officer at the Royal Astronomical Society, and she is also a secondary school Science teacher. She told me, 'When I teach, I've had young girls say to me, "You don't look like a scientist. You're young and Indian, and a woman . . ." It's so important for them to see it to believe it, to shatter their preconceptions.' That's precisely why Sheila and her sister Nikki set up STEMMsisters, to connect, inspire and empower young women who need support in STEMM fields. This is something that organizations like The Girls' Network are also striving for. They recognize that under-represented minorities, in particular, might be faced with a limited role model pool outside of their families, so the mentees are paired up with a positive, relatable role model. It can be life-changing for a brown girl, having a woman of colour who can provide you with the cultural and social capital they've developed over the years, introduce you to their networks and provide you with career guidance. Someone who won't feed that melodramatic construction that brown girls possess limited agency because of the parental restrictions and cultural expectations on them, and instead empathize with the complex nuances to a brown girl's decision-making process.

## A divided self?

Surely the 'between two cultures' discourse is starting to get a bit dated now? My generation's reality is far from that. Rather than seeing brown girls being stuck between West vs East, civilized/uncivilized, traditional/modern, oppressed/liberated, and the veiled/unveiled woman, it's about time we move away from this outdated binary model and recognize that we can accommodate multiple ways of being and performing brown womanhood. Brown women are the ultimate code-switchers, and we know how to do it with ease. For example, a brown woman can be independent, but still stay connected to her family. She can be a leader in the workplace without rejecting her culture. Our understanding of 'freedom' and 'success' may be very different from that of the white Western world, but that does not mean it is less valid. We are active negotiators in our life trajectory, rather than passive subjects.

When I was coming to the end of my undergraduate degree in history, I began applying for a master's degree in courses related to gender studies and sociology. My time as an undergrad had spurred my passion for intersectional feminism, and I knew I wanted to learn more in an academic space. I applied to some of the top universities in London, but also decided to give Oxford and Cambridge a go. When I was applying for my undergraduate degree three years earlier, I'd never thought I was a likely Oxbridge candidate, so I'd never even considered it. But now my self-confidence and self-belief had grown, and I was intrigued to find out whether I was able to get in or not. Imagine my pleasure when a few weeks later, I received acceptance letters from both Oxford and Cambridge. However, deep down I knew that if I accepted the offer, it would mean moving out of my family home. A daily commute from east London to either of those places would take up most of my day.

At the time, my elder siblings were already married and had flown the nest, and my other brother was away on a placement year. If I had gone away to Oxford, my parents and elderly grandparents would have been left alone just at a time when their health requirements meant that they needed extra support. I took the decision, by myself, to reject the offers. I never spoke to my parents about it. At the time, I felt like I didn't want to give them the emotional burden. In hindsight, maybe I should have told them, just because I now know that communication is key to any relationship. But it wouldn't have changed my decision. Did it make me any less of an empowered feminist because I made this choice? Of course not. Did it make me any less 'successful'? Definitely not. I still went to a fantastic Russell Group university, one of the best in the world, in fact, and more recently I ended up on a leadership programme at Oxford University anyway. But what this moment made me realize is that there is an extra variable in a brown girl's decision-making process – not always verbalized, not always a conscious one, but it is there, nevertheless. And a brown woman shouldn't be seen as any 'lesser' just because we have these other variables (such as our family, faith and culture) to consider.

But being seen as 'lesser' and not being able to tell our story has been ingrained in all aspects of our lives, from how we are presented in mainstream media to how we are treated in schools. Do we need a larger shift in the education system to take place, from primary school all the way through to higher education – and beyond – until we're seen as more? Hell, yeah! But where do we start? Perhaps we'll start with what we are, or should I say what we aren't, being taught about ourselves.

## *The whitewashing of education*

In school, I grew up hearing about Florence Nightingale, but never about Mary Mahoney. I'd heard of George Orwell but never Arundhati Roy. Emmeline Pankhurst but never Sophia Duleep Singh. The systemic suppression of non-European culture and history in education may not seem important, but it is a part of the same ethos which permits the everyday culture of ethnic minority life to be totally ignored in schools. If we had a national curriculum that included more of our history, could this impact our long-term prospects in life? Would this help give us a sense of confidence in our identity? Would I, as a brown woman, feel like I had more of a voice? If our national curriculum included the injustices of the British Empire, perhaps this would reduce the amount of racial and cultural insensitivity that takes place in our society. The same would be true if we had an education system that included the stories and voices of migration from the South Asian continent during the decolonization period.

When I was studying history in school, we were told nothing of the concentration camps the British army ran during the Boer War, or the Bengal famine of 1943, or the massacres of Kenyans in the 1950s or the Amritsar Massacre in 1919. These are things my dad taught me. Sometimes I wonder whether if my dad hadn't encouraged my love for history, I would have pursued it. He used to have amazing books lying around the house, history books from all around the world, philosophy books by Asian and African thinkers, atlases and maps, and not just the famous Mercator projection that we see in all classrooms. As my dad used to say, 'There is no excuse for ignorance with a house full of books and a library card.' Those words still ring true in my mind to this day.

When I think about the short stories I used to write as a child, my characters would always be white. Hannah and Sarah used to be my go-to names, I'm not quite sure why. They had blonde hair and blue eyes and they ate 'English food'. It was the only story I knew how to tell because it was the only story I saw.

In the words of award-winning Nigerian author Chimamanda Ngozi Adichie, author of *We Should All Be Feminists*, 'The single story creates stereotypes, and the problem with stereotypes is not that they are untrue, but that they are incomplete. They make one story become the only story.' That is why Sheila, who I mentioned earlier, wanted to make sure that her books *How to be an Astronaut* and *Space on Earth* were illustrated with a child of colour on the cover. The issue runs deeper when we look at the writers behind the books. In the 2019 Book Trust Report, Dr Melanie Ramdarshan Bold found that in 2017, only 5.6 per cent of published authors and illustrators in the UK were people of colour (and of that, only 1.98 per cent were British born) and that between 2007 and 2017, white children's book creators had around twice as many books published compared to those of colour. These writers have also talked about feeling pigeonholed, and the difficulties in simply 'being creators' without talking about their ethnicity, or issues relating to it, within or outside of their books. Sadly, like most industries, publishing is a market-driven industry. If books by writers of colour or with characters of colour aren't selling, then publishers can suggest there's no need for them. So, get out there and buy books by black and brown authors, find the books with characters of colour, buy five copies, or ten, talk about them, write about them and give them to all the children you know.

Reading is a fundamental part of any childhood, not only intellectually to support literacy skills, but also emotionally as a way to develop cognitive thinking. Seeing, or should I say reading, about characters that are like you can make a massive impact on a child's self-esteem and even deepen their love for reading. And for young white readers, it would also encourage a sense of cultural understanding and empathy for others. But this was never the case when I was growing up, and still isn't. The Centre for Literacy in Primary Education found that only 7 per cent of children's books published in Britain in 2018 had a Black, Asian or minority ethnic character, despite the fact that this exact demographic makes up a third of school-age children. When these characters do appear, they are very rarely the protagonist, often only a sidekick or characterized purely by their ethnicity.

The national curriculum which was introduced under Margaret Thatcher in the 1980s is still pretty much what we are using today. The history specification was, and still is, one of the most contested areas. The curriculum's 'compulsory' content was stripped back, with detailed bullet points that were previously listed as mandatory now presented as suggestions. Empire is indeed on this list and is introduced when students start secondary school. But it's essentially up to the school, or in this case, the History department and teachers, precisely what and how things are taught. Some teachers might spend a single lesson on it. Some might spend up to six weeks on it (half a term).

Author and historian Dr Priya Atwal looked into school textbook history in her awesome radio show *Lies My Teacher Told Me* on BBC Radio 4. She investigated how much textbooks can reveal about a nation's desire to shape or avoid the complexities of its own past. When she invited me on the show, I highlighted that here in the UK, the textbook curriculum discussion is a little more complicated when you realize that academies and free schools now make up 75 per cent of secondary schools,[6] none of which are bound to the curriculum.

Regarding the listed teaching suggestions, it's not the teacher's fault if they pick the topics they are most familiar with or have studied themselves. Sadly, this results in a vicious cycle of whitewashed history being taught over and over again. An investigation by the *Guardian* found that only a fifth of UK universities are willing to consider decolonizing the curriculum.[7] After seeing the findings, Professor Kalwant Bhopal, the director of the Centre for Research in Race and Education at Birmingham University, said that 'every university should have this as a priority. If it's not in the strategic plan, it's not considered important to the university.' So, if it's not a priority at universities either, how will we have teachers equipped with the subject knowledge necessary to teach it in schools? This whole cycle makes my head spin.

Nav Sanghara, an executive headteacher for the Inspire Partnership, also pointed out the importance of 'oracy, talk and presenting across the curriculum from an early age'. She told me this would allow students to 'work on identity and valuing self so that they can express or at least start articulating what they are proud of about themselves or what they find challenging.' Perhaps this is something that should also be considered in curriculum changes, and something that I know would really benefit our brown girls and their confidence in public speaking and owning their voice in a room.

## *Mirror, mirror*

We need a curriculum in which children can see reflections of themselves. Not only will they start to feel more in tune with themselves, more confident and able to develop a strong sense of self-actualization, but they will also do better academically if they are engaged. Brown girls will be more enthusiastic about entering classroom discussions when they feel it actually relates to them. As History teacher Shalina pointed out: 'Is the only place South Asian girls see themselves in the curriculum during PHSE discussions of forced marriage? Or by seeing the occasional photo of Malala on a PowerPoint slide. This is a problem!'

Historically, school assemblies have usually been a safe space to explore and challenge inequality, and a great opportunity to bring in specialist guest speakers from a diverse number of fields. Nineteen-year-old Kruti Jani, a mentee of The Girls' Network from Wembley, told me: 'In my school there were a lot of talks held where there would be external speakers that would come in to talk about their career path. Personally, I felt really inspired.' I've often been asked to go into schools with a high demographic of brown girls to share inspiring stories about brown women and to help boost their aspirations. But this should be a supplement to a broader teaching, not the only place this happens. The consideration of race and racism, and how this can differ in accordance to gender and class, needs to be embedded across the school ethos. Subjects like PHSE, English, religious studies and sociology provide a space to tackle some of these topics. Still, even subjects like maths and science have the opportunity to be more inclusive. There are amazing teachers across the country, some of whom are in this book, who are trying to engage with these issues and are attempting to provide an accessible and relatable education to all. Which leads me to wonder, if we don't have teachers of colour or teachers with racial literacy pushing for this ethos to be implemented in schools, how will it happen?

According to the government's national statistics, in 2018, of all teachers in state-funded schools in England, only around 14 per cent were from ethnic minorities, falling way below the 32 per cent of the pupil population who come from ethnic minority groups.[8] This issue became particularly relevant in 2020 and 2021, when GCSEs and A-level exams were cancelled due to the COVID-19 pandemic. This left the awarding of grades to the teachers, relying on previous assessments and attainment records. Was there a danger of under-awarding brown girls because of our preconceived notions about them? Was there anyone in the school raising this concern, or considering the nuances that apply to grade predictions and ethnicity?

Having teachers who are representative of the local community's socio-cultural backgrounds might mean parents of ethnic minority backgrounds would be more likely to communicate with them in times of need. It's also important for white students to see diversity represented in aspirational and professional positions within their school, perhaps to challenge any unconscious biases they may adopt growing up. We need these teachers at all levels. Parents, and even some teachers, too often expect to find a tall, white, male headteacher waiting at the school gates. This is the image of a strong leader and position of authority that society has conditioned us to expect. That's not surprising when we see that in 2019, 97.1 per cent of male headteachers and 96.2 per cent of female headteachers were white.[9] But women like Bushra Nasir, the first Muslim female headteacher in the UK, completely shatter that perception. Bushra held over twenty years of experience at her school in Newham and was awarded TES Headteacher of the Year in summer 2012, when she retired. Women like Bushra and Dr Saima Rana, principal of Westminster Academy, have served in some of the most deprived areas in the country, and recognize that raising the confidence and aspirations of young girls is vital if we want our brown girls to excel beyond the classroom.

We need to be increasing the number of trainee teachers coming in from a diverse number of backgrounds and, equally important, retaining them. The Big Question Survey carried out by the National Association of Schoolmasters Union of Women Teachers (NASUWT) in 2016 found that around 31 per cent of teachers of colour experienced discrimination in the workplace. A whopping 79 per cent of them believed that they were not paid at a level 'commensurate with their skills and experiences'. It doesn't end there – nearly two-thirds of them had experienced 'verbal abuse by pupils'. That makes me feel heartbroken. No wonder so many of them don't stay in the profession. We need to be going even further than just retaining them, we need to be protecting them and supporting them so that we have more black and brown teachers in the classroom to push for and support the needs of marginalized communities. That being said, it shouldn't *just* be them raising the alarm. As if we haven't got enough on our plates already. A teacher of colour may get pigeonholed as the teacher who is the expert on 'race' or 'gender' issues, forced to become the spokesperson for all-things-diversity, further 'othering' their experience. It shouldn't just be on the teachers of colour to carry the emotional burden and put in the extra hours to find the resources and create diverse schemes of work.

## Racial literacy

It was around the time I was doing my GCSEs, and my friend and I were making our way out of our form room towards the canteen to grab some lunch. Approaching us from the other side of the corridor was a teacher who would always stop us for a uniform check. I always loved, and still do, big hooped earrings, and tried my best to sneakily remove them from my ears before the teacher got any closer. But it was too late. 'Hand them over, Jaspreet,' she said. It was the second confiscation that week. There's probably still a collection of my big hooped earrings in a drawer somewhere. The teacher then looked to my friend and said, 'There is a strict no-make-up policy, you know that. What would your family say about you wearing make-up and a head-scarf?' My friend and I looked at each other, baffled. 'Isn't your headscarf for you to look modest? Your make-up is drawing attention to yourself, isn't it? Either the headscarf or make-up, you can't do both.'

Now let's unpack what had just happened. My friend was expected to perform being an 'authentic' Muslim in the eyes of this teacher. Essentially, my friend was being told how she, as a Muslim, should or should not behave according to the expectations of someone who wasn't even a Muslim themselves. Yes, there was a strict no-jewellery and no-make-up policy which applied to everyone, but the problem was how this teacher had singled out and shamed my friend in relation to her religion. Her assumptions were based on her understanding that Muslim girls who transcended traditionally or ethnically prescribed religious and cultural boundaries were performing two incompatible identities. She, a white middle-class woman in a position of power, was defining what constitutes a good practising Muslim girl. But who was she to keep my Muslim friend's identity in check like that? Interestingly, the pressure of being a 'good girl' is worse for brown girls whose teachers see them as transcending cultural boundaries, and who are often labelled as more disruptive. This policing and surveillance of our performance as brown girls, especially by white people in authority, is confusing, exhausting and dangerous.

This focus on racial literacy would allow teachers to pay greater attention to brown girls' cultural background in more individualized ways and not see them as one homogenous group. More racial literacy in schools would avoid situations like the one I experienced.

As we're on the topic of school uniform, this is probably a good place to talk about skirts. Since 2018, there has been an ongoing conversation about the UK's school uniform policy. There is currently no overarching policy, and it is usually left to the school's discretion. But for years, female students have been asking why boys and teachers can wear trousers, but they can't. At least forty secondary schools have banned girls from wearing skirts, favouring a gender-neutral uniform for everyone. Some argue that it's less about banning skirts altogether, and more, importantly, about telling young women – all young women – they have an element of choice. This has been a much longer battle for brown women, whose families may not have been comfortable with them wearing skirts. I had students who'd have to get changed on their way to school or on the way out, because their parents were uncomfortable with them wearing a skirt, but it was the school's policy. If we advocated for an element of choice between skirts and trousers, we would be creating a safer space for brown bodies too.

This has been a long fight for brown women. Back in 1981, nineteen-year-old Tajwinder Kaur was training to become a nurse in south-west London. In February of that year, Tajwinder objected to being forced to wear a skirt as part of the nurse uniform. She said she'd be willing to wear trousers underneath the skirt, but at the tribunal, the health authority refused to compromise. That June, Tajwinder took her case to the Court of Appeal, where they eventually agreed she could wear trousers and she was offered a place on the next training course starting in October. She told *The Times* 'I am very happy with the outcome. But I would have preferred not to have gone through with all this. After a year's delay to my career, we have arrived at the solution which I proposed in the first place.' What a revolutionary moment for nurses, and for women across the UK. But her story has gone unheard. 'This was a clear case of indirect discrimination, even if unintentional.' Fast forward to the present day, and we're still having the same discussions in schools. Again, we brown girls are tired.

Anti-racism is a job for everyone. Racial literacy is crucial across all areas of society, from the private sector to the public sector and everything in between. Implementing these values at the heart of the education sector will compel and empower teachers to engage with uncomfortable discussions around white privilege and white power structures for the betterment of all children. There's no point having educational manifestos that claim 'every child matters', 'bridge the gap' and 'no child left behind' when there is no commitment to these slogans. It needs to be more than performative.

A whole-school, institutionalized approach is critical. Schools need to consider their policies, and place issues relating to gender and ethnicity on the same level as safeguarding and health and safety concerns. And these policies need to be consistent across all schools, both in rural areas and cities. This is especially important when you consider that many brown women live in some of the country's most deprived areas. Without these policies, it is difficult for students, parents and teachers to raise any concerns about welfare. Brown parents might feel they'll be perceived as 'troublemakers' if they have concerns that their child is being bullied. Brown teachers might feel worried about being treated differently if they highlight their experiences of discrimination. A child might feel no one will believe them. The June 2020 Runnymede Report highlighted the misguided and incoherent school policies on anti-racism, noting that even 'a high-profile BME headteacher' advised parents to ignore young people's claims of racism. 'If [a] child says [a] teacher is being racist, back the teacher. Whatever the child says, back the teacher . . . If you don't, you are letting the child down and allowing them to play you for a fool.' We all know how dangerous this kind of rhetoric can be when we don't allow the victim to convey their side of the story . . .

Instead, the government still requires schools to uphold problematic policies like teaching 'British Values' (whatever the hell that means) and implementing the 'Prevent strategy', which requires 'staff to identify children who may be vulnerable to radicalization'. Both of these policies enforce a sense of cultural supremacism, and they directly impact brown children, specifically Muslim children, in schools that further marginalize them. It highlights how one's 'difference' could be a threat. In her article for the *Guardian*, educator, poet and writer Suhaiymah Manzoor-Khan, emphasized how the policy has been 'repeatedly condemned for enabling racial profiling'. We need to make sure that any policies that ratify themes of cultural supremacism and Islamophobia, whether overtly or covertly, are stripped out of the classroom. At the very least they should be appropriately reviewed before we marginalize even more brown children.

Clearer school policies on inequality and discrimination that do not marginalize students (or staff for that matter) are becoming more and more crucial. I remember once hearing a student say to another girl in the class that she smelt like 'a Paki'. I sent her out of the classroom, and a senior member of staff said she'd handle it. When I went to the meeting with the senior leader and the student after I finished teaching my lesson, the teacher told me that it had not been a racial slur and that 'Paki' was, in fact, the name of a perfume. The student even pitched in, telling me, 'You can buy it at Selfridges, you probably wouldn't know.' And it was left at that. No further discussion. Written off. I genuinely thought maybe I was in the wrong! I even went to the extent of googling 'Paki perfume' to see if it was real. Can you believe it? The student happily skipped away. At the time, I was less concerned about the power play that took place in that meeting and more worried about the life lesson we had just taught that child: how you can get away with racism by pleading ignorance. In the whole situation, I wasn't even mad at the student, I was more upset with the other teacher and the general overt denial, used to silence me. I decided to take things into my own hands and focused more of my lessons on the history of immigration for the rest of the term. I never heard a comment like that from the student again. In fact at the end of the school year she wrote me a letter apologizing for all the times she had misbehaved and called me her favourite teacher. Maybe there is hope after all.

The need for racial literacy and radical changes to policies also applies to higher education. But as we saw earlier, not many universities concern themselves with this, and some are even in denial that this kind of racism even exists. Many South Asian girls are the first in their families to go to university. For many brown women, including myself, it is the first time they might notice their 'otherness' and how whiteness and white privilege dominate the space within those ivory towers. The percentage of brown girls going to university has been steadily increasing year by year, and it's well documented that they achieve better than average academic qualifications, but they still remain under-represented in Russell Group universities. It's often the case that teachers don't encourage even the brightest brown girls to apply to the top universities, especially Oxbridge, just because statistically they are less likely to get in.

## Taking the roads less travelled

So, until these educational institutions improve, what can we do within our communities so that brown girls are excelling? Would it help to encourage our brown girls to explore less 'traditional' career choices? Yes, auntie, it's OK if your daughter doesn't want to become a doctor-lawyer-accountant-dentist. Of course, these are highly respected professions, but as Diksha Bent (who worked as a drama teacher and head of year in a mixed comprehensive school in Uxbridge) pointed out, '. . . South Asian families focus on financial stability and therefore project career paths onto their children which in their minds allow them to achieve that. Being financially independent allows greater autonomy over one's subsequent choices, however, at what cost?' The stereotypical definition of success constructed within immigrant cultures is costing us our representation in fields such as the humanities, social sciences, entrepreneurship and the arts.

Also, as great as becoming a doctor-lawyer-accountant-dentist is, these professions are highly competitive. The intense demand for places means more of a struggle to get in, which can apply even more pressure and unnecessary anxiety to young brown girls. It's also expensive, as these fields require ongoing training. Let me also emphasize here that university is not for everyone. Other future pathways, including apprenticeships or internships, volunteering or maybe taking a gap year and doing work experience in different industries, are just as valid. Diksha found that many of her South Asian students who didn't attain 8 A*–Cs found themselves working in nurseries or in retail. She said, 'I don't think there is anything wrong with any of these professions, I just feel that South Asian girls are presented with such limited options that when they don't fit the mould and have the academic success that is expected of them, their futures are limited.' And here lies one of my most important pieces of advice. You are not limited, so why should your life choices be?

You don't need one set plan, you don't need to follow just one career path or tick just one box. Tick all of them! I knew I loved studying history, so there lay my choice to study history as an undergrad. That led to my passion for feminism, and there lay my choice to pursue gender studies as a postgraduate. From there, I wanted to be a teacher, but I also wanted to be a poet and a writer. One day I would love to write and make films. One day I might be an astronaut! Just look at Swati Mohan, the woman behind NASA's first successfully landed Perseverance rover on Mars in February 2021 (and she was rocking a bindi in the control room)! OK, so maybe I'm not going to be an astronaut, but you get me. Living a life filled with a sense of purpose and passion, doing the things that feel worth waking up for, that's what we should be encouraging in our brown girls so that they can excel.

Having representation in different fields will benefit the community in so many ways. Not only will it provide us with a voice in these spaces but also a chance to take hold of our narrative and how our stories are told. Imagine more brown girl researchers. Imagine more brown girl actors. Imagine more brown girl journalists. Filmmakers. Entrepreneurs. Developers. Engineers. The list is endless! That's why I take my students with me to the Asian Women of Achievement Awards each year. I won the Arts and Culture category back in 2017 and am now an alumnus and ambassador for the award's Women of the Future Programme. I wanted to take my brown girl students with me so that they could hear the incredible stories of the women nominated that year, ranging from CEOs to Olympic medallists. I wanted them to see they can truly be whatever they want to be, despite the barriers they may face along the way because of their gender or the colour of their skin.

And it is important that we prepare them for those barriers. When they do step into the world of work, things may get even harder. While we women of colour have unequivocally entered the workplace, we are still not deemed equal in that space. They will be entering a territorial, fraternal and sometimes aggressive realm, one in which they'll have to manage microaggressions on a daily basis. Don't you worry, the next chapter will get us fully equipped for how to handle that.

What I would also love to see is the development of liberatory education that encourages critical enquiry. The kind of education that encourages debate, dialogue and discussion and space where young people can engage in their education in a meaningful way. Liberatory education, sometimes known as transgressive education, encourages disruptive thinking. And that's what brown girls need, the willingness to disrupt. This practice of teaching also looks at how we consider growth in our mind, body and soul. I might sound like a complete hippie (which I'm fine with, by the way), but hear me out. I hope that the knowledge we provide can enhance and nourish us in our spiritual growth just as much as our academic growth. As seminal feminist and social activist bell hooks noted in her work *Teaching to Transgress: Education as the Practice of Freedom*, 'there is an aspect of our vocation that is sacred; our work is not merely to share information but to share in the intellectual and spiritual growth of our students.' She argues that this 'union of mind, body, and spirit' is possible in the classroom, but 'most of my professors were not the slightest bit interested in enlightenment. More than anything they seemed enthralled by the exercise of power and authority within their mini-kingdom, the classroom.' This is a problem affecting all schoolchildren, of course. Our education system is focused on a very Western ideal of retaining information, memorizing facts, rather than getting young people to truly think critically – to start thinking critically about what we see and what we don't see. This implicitly discourages independent thought and any challenges to the status quo.

Sadly, the blueprint on how we can do better for brown girls isn't a simple one. It's not as simple as throwing more people of colour onto the curriculum or having more brown teachers in the classroom. Cuts have had significant consequences for ethnic minority students and teachers, as there is less space to talk about race or address racial literacy, let alone look at the issues through a more complex lens. So, until we see a radical shift in our education system, how about we decentre these institutions, schools and universities, as the only way to gain legitimate knowledge? How about we work on brown girl empowerment and education? How about we recentre ourselves as agents of our own encouragement and learning?

## It starts with us

As brown women, we have the most influential role to play in transforming how we, as brown women, see ourselves, and we all must become active participants in this shift. We must make a deliberate effort. How can we use our own voices, our own positions of privilege, to self-educate but also to re-educate? I'm tired of white men writing about themselves or writing about us. We should be our own experts. Shouldn't we be trying to fill the gaps in our knowledge, and looking for all the things that the textbooks didn't teach us? Access to knowledge and education doesn't just have to be in a classroom. It can be found in the books that we read, the stories we are told and now, with the power of the digital age, the knowledge is at our fingertips. If you're a student, could you be holding lunchtime discussions, book clubs or setting up your own university society for a brown sisterhood to encourage a space for dialogue? For brown women slightly further on in their journey, could you join a mentoring network and become a mentor for young brown girls in your area to support them on their journey? Could you go into your local school to provide talks and assemblies? Could you be doing more to support the brown girls in your family? Let's show them and ourselves all that we can be.

Our revolution goes beyond the classroom. Our revolution has been burning inside us all along. The knowledge and power we were searching for were with us all along. We just have to learn it and love it. That self-love will keep us stable even when we have to code-switch, even when we have to negotiate expectations within the home and within the classroom, even when people think brown girls only have the dream of getting married and have no other aspirations in life. In the words of bell hooks, 'if we give our children sound self-love, they will be able to deal with whatever life puts before them.'

# CHAPTER 3

# THAT'S NOT MY NAME

*Managing Microaggressions*

they call me 'her'
they call me 'jas'
that's not my name, that's not my name
that's not my name, that's not my name

when you say my name
say it whole for me
because i'm tired of only being half of me
so that the other kids wouldn't laugh at me
it's easier for you to pronounce
but the sounds are no longer mine
and the meaning is becoming more difficult to define
i'm renamed
maybe it's me who's too lenient
i folded up my name into a small box that will roll off your tongue
to be more convenient
until my syllables are simply fragments of east vs west
is this me at my best?
. . . if i'm only half of me.

**that's not my name**

t's your first lesson of a new school year. Jonathan . . . Check. Jessica . . . Check. Jackie . . . Check. Jaz . . . ? You take in a deep inhale and sigh, as you've seen this scrunched-up face of confusion before. Before her lips begin to part, you start to deliberate over whether you should repeat the accurate pronunciation of your name, at the expense of drawing attention to yourself in front of your new class, or sit there and do nothing. It doesn't seem like that big a deal but, as many of us know, it is. Sometimes conforming is the easier and often safer path to take. Hanan becomes 'Hannah', Nikhila becomes 'Niki', Feroza becomes Frozen or, occasionally and casually, a whole new name is created. Jaspreet often became Jazdeep, Jasmine, or – my personal favourite – Jasper . . . I never corrected them, and I know there are thousands of other brown girls who have done the same. This isn't just limited to South Asian names. But what are we losing every time this happens?

Our names hold ancestral and historical significance. When they are mispronounced, changed or shortened to conform to Western norms, these actions eradicate the meaning behind them. That transition is often painful and forces many students to adopt names that are not their own. I've lost count of the times I have told people to just call me 'Jas' to make it easier for them. For the children of immigrants or those who have

English as an additional language (EAL learners), a teacher who knows their name and pronounces it correctly signals respect, and this marks a critical step in developing their self-confidence. I've seen this first-hand in the schools where I have taught. A mispronounced name is often the first of many slights that these children experience in classrooms and, as we saw in the last chapter, these students are already unlikely to see educators who look like them, teachers who speak their language, or a curriculum that reflects their culture. Rita Kohli, Associate Professor in the Education, Society and Culture Program at the University of California's Graduate School of Education, found that having your name mispronounced can also hinder academic progress. She explains that this is one of the many microaggressions that can emerge in a classroom and seriously undermine learning. 'Names have incredible significance to families, with so much thought, meaning and culture woven into them,' Kohli says. 'When the child enters school and teachers – consciously or not – mispronounce, disregard or change the name, they are in a sense disregarding the family and culture of the students as well . . . Students often felt shame, embarrassment and that their name was a burden [. . .] They often began to shy away from their language, culture and families.'[1]

Over time, we brown women even become conditioned to apologizing to the world for any confusion the name might cause. 'Sorry, it's Jaspreet.' But why am I the one apologizing when it's my name that's being butchered? If my mother had to exercise her vocal cords daily to whisper out her broken English, then you can exercise yours, too. Of course, it's OK to have a nickname, shorten your name, or have a whole new name entirely, if that's what *you* want. My brothers call me Jas from time to time, and so do some of my friends, but only after asking for my permission. Brown girls shouldn't feel the need to shorten and/or change their names in order to become closer to whiteness. A lifetime of mispronunciations, misspellings and outright refusals to attempt my 'difficult' name led me to be ashamed of what my dad had gifted me with. I gave myself other nicknames in school, Jaz, JP, Lady S . . . Yeah, let's not go there. I always wanted to have the kind of name you could find on one those keyrings in a gift shop.

For me, halving my name to just 'Jas' was one of the many examples of attempting to make myself smaller. More palatable. More unseen. Comedian and actor Emily Lloyd-Saini has shared her experiences of having a Western name in a brown body through her comedic work. Growing up with Welsh-Indian heritage in the small town of Sandiacre in the East Midlands, she described on a BBC Sounds podcast, *No Country for Young Women*, that 'Sandiacre was the kind of town where you walk into a Starbucks and they'd be like *makes scared expression* . . . "What's your name?" And as soon as I'd say Emily, they'd be like "Thank God!"' So, here's a little advice. If you're ever afraid you can't pronounce a person's name, just ask them how they would like it to be pronounced – it's not that hard. It might feel a little awkward at first, but it's not as awkward as being made to feel your name is too unfamiliar to be spoken properly. If you can pronounce Leonardo DiCaprio, you can pronounce Jaspreet. Let's be real: we're not always going to get people's names right. But, more than ever, it matters that you try.

## *Those comments cut deep*

This mispronunciation of names is just one of many micro-aggressions that ethnic minorities have to deal with on a daily basis. Imagine a microaggression as a tiny paper cut. When it first happens, it stings, but you won't bleed to death. But imagine getting ten paper cuts a day, your hands would really start to hurt. By the tenth paper cut, you'd be fuming! Imagine then when you start talking about the pain, you are gaslit and told, 'Come on, it's only a paper cut.' Little can they see, you're covered in them. The perceived smallness of the action can make microaggressions all the more sinister. But there is nothing micro about microaggressions. They creep into the workplace and into society in general and open the door to further dismissal of our identities as brown women. Like many of the buzzwords that have surfaced in recent years, the true meaning of microaggressions gets diluted or, worse still, ignored completely. But that doesn't erase how truly harmful they can be. The term was first coined by Harvard professor Chester M. Price, in the 1970s, and was later developed by psychologists like Derald Wing Sue and his team in the early 2000s. Sue recognized how important it was to name, detail and classify the types of micro-aggressions that occur in everyday life for marginalized communities.[2] These include microassaults, which are 'explicit racial derogations characterised primarily by a verbal or nonverbal attack meant to hurt the intended victim through name-calling, avoidant behaviour, or purposeful discriminatory actions.' These are usually deliberate. Examples include calling someone a Paki, referring to people as 'coloured' even now, or serving a white person in a restaurant before a brown person.

There are also microinsults, which 'demean a person's racial heritage or identity'. These are the more subtle ones, like 'will you have to get an arranged marriage?', 'your lunches are always so different!' or 'what does your hair look like under your scarf?'. And finally, Sue pointed out that there are also microinvalidations. These types of microaggression usually nullify or 'other' the recipient. I get these a lot when I'm told I 'speak so well!' or the oh-so-famous 'where are you *really* from?' question. Research shows that these racial microaggressions are having a devastating impact on our self-esteem.[3] All these paper cuts are eroding brown women's mental health, job performance, career progression and the quality of their social experience.

The impact these implicit biases have on young Asian women is clear, especially on those from Pakistani and Bangladeshi backgrounds. According to the Office for National Statistics, as of 2018, women from the Pakistani community had an 'inactivity rate' (meaning they were not in the labour force) of 54.5 per cent and Bangladeshi women of 57.8 per cent, over double that of White British women.[4] This has often been put down to 'cultural differences in the dynamics of the family unit'. But has anyone stopped to consider that this also might be down to the working world not feeling like a welcoming and safe space for them? Not everything comes down to cultural differences. The workplace could be somewhere they would have to consistently consider their own outward performance, rehearsing and rehearsing every single day. Another notable finding was that in 2018, the largest pay gap between men and women was in the Indian ethnic group, with Indian men earning 23.3 per cent more per hour than Indian women.[5] A brown woman's place in the working world is very different to that of her male counterparts. Yes, we may face similar racialized forms of oppression, but intertwine that with existing patriarchal and misogynistic structures and hierarchies, and you've got one hell of a shit show. Why is nobody questioning these things?

It's also important to consider that the number of well-off brown women is still pretty small. Yet these are often the women who are prominent on race-relations committees and hold dialogue in spaces of power, highlighting the problems they think brown women face without always knowing their perspective. It is still very rare to find working-class brown women in these spaces. And that's a big problem.

COCo (the Centre for Community Organizations) is a charitable organization that has been looking into the experience of women of colour in the workplace. They revealed that when a woman of colour enters an organization, invariably run by white leadership, they initially feel welcomed and appreciated. This is known as the 'honeymoon period'. After a little while – and this can vary from days to months – the woman may start to experience a number of covert microaggressions. COCo states these could be 'heightened surveillance of her work and interpersonal relationships, repeated comments about her body and physical presentation and expectations of her addressing internal race dynamics'.[6] If she decides to flag up these issues, it's often she who becomes the problem. Sooner or later, she's either asked to resign, she quits or goes on sick leave. It's not unusual for the woman of colour to tell her employer that she's going on sick leave for health reasons unrelated to the discrimination, even if that is the real reason, just to avoid confrontation.

I never recognized these as microaggressions when I first stepped into the working world. If anything, I was often put up on a pedestal, tokenized if you will. I would be put forward for roles (unpaid, I might add), and I thought I was being appreciated and promoted. I was put on the cover of leaflets and used for marketing material. Little did I know, my race, my gender and my qualifications were, in fact, being used against me. I never realized that microaggressions could be coded in that way. I thought, 'How kind, they think I'm wonderful!' When in fact it wasn't an acknowledgement of my skills, I was being fetishized. Not having other people similar to me to bounce these thoughts off was what made it so difficult. Is this behaviour acceptable? It was all new to me. I had seen how fetishization could play out in more obvious ways, like being called exotic or, my other notable favourite, Princess Jasmine . . . But I didn't know a woman of colour could be fetishized like that in the workplace.

By the way, the Princess Jasmine-related microaggressions still arrive in my inboxes, usually, I am sorry to say, from middle-aged white men. Gross, I know. I'm not a bloody mango or a fairy tale princess. And if anything, I'd rather be the mango. The concept has derived from the colonial ideal that women of colour, especially Asian and black women, should be sexually available to white men in positions of power and privilege. Brown women are often desexualized and sexualized at the same time. On the one hand, we are desexualized by our own communities, encouraged to avoid desire and exploring our sexuality, which leads to feeling unsexy in our brown bodies and hinders our self-esteem. Simultaneously, historically we have been exoticized by the white man for our 'submissive' and 'obedient' nature. And essentially, the workplace is doing the same thing, just in a different way; using our 'submissive' and 'obedient' nature to make sure that the work is done, and done well. We are then made hyper-visible in order to tick their diversity box obsession, which does nothing but present an outward image of diversity and inclusion.

This hyper-visibility is something that brown women have to navigate in the workplace on a daily basis, and that impacts our mental wellbeing. To feel seen, yet also unseen. Lecturer and author Nirmal Puwar suggested in her work *Space Invaders: Race, Gender and Bodies Out of Place*, that this type of hyper-visibility causes a 'super-surveillance [. . .] the tiniest error in a performance can be picked up and amplified as proof of the person not being quite up to the job [. . .] Undue pressure can itself induce mistakes which are indicative of the anxiety and nervousness produced, rather than of the actual abilities of the person under scrutiny.' If you are being watched all the time, this feeling of hyper-visibility might mean you're more likely to make mistakes. Being watched like this is a microaggression, and can add to our own nervousness and sense of imposter syndrome. A brown woman's reputation is more likely to be tarnished because of this. For a white man, for instance, there is less likely to be a sense of constant surveillance, and there is a power that comes with that type of invisibility.

To add to my own sense of this hyper-visibility, I am a tall brown woman. At 5ft 10in, I am almost 6ft with shoes on. For years I was so ashamed of my height. I would hunch my shoulders in and even crouch slightly when standing, in the hope of feeling smaller. I'm still trying to unlearn my terrible posture to this day. I did the same with my heritage, identity and the colour of my skin. I wanted to make it smaller and less seen. But this was impossible and, over time, I realized I didn't have to. If I was going to be this visible, I had to own it.

## Being brown and British

Another common microaggression, one that brown millennials especially seem to receive, is being told, usually in a shocked and almost congratulatory tone, how articulate we are. But what does this actually signal to us? Is it that the use of good vocabulary and grammar is usually associated with whiteness, and our speech has confused their perception of that? For years I was worried about hiding my east London accent under my tongue, now I have to worry about this? I shouldn't have to 'sound white' in order to have a competent, intellectual conversation. I should be able to have a competent, intellectual conversation by sounding like me. And anyway, there is no such thing as 'sounding white'. I am articulate by sounding like me. In fact, many brown women are articulate in multiple languages, not just in English. Try being articulate in Urdu, Punjabi, Hindi, Tamil and Bengali, like many of our mums are. If you ever do want to compliment a person of colour, commend them on *what* they said, perhaps a specific idea or insight they provided, or what they taught you. Commenting on how someone speaks really isn't necessary.

The microaggressions can sometimes be way more explicit than this. For example, Joyti, whom we met in the last chapter, told me that when she worked for a top footwear retail brand, a team member asked, 'What type of Asian are you? Are you like the ones in *Bend It Like Beckham* or *East is East*, because I don't like those ones . . .' Whether you've watched the two movies or not, the problem lies in the fact that Joyti's fellow white employee was making ignorant assumptions about her that reduced her to either one of two stereotypes. Similarly, a Pakistani friend of mine, who would like to stay anonymous, was asked, 'So which

Muslim are you? Do you fast? Or do you celebrate Christmas?' Other examples include, 'I didn't realize Asians could get sunburnt' or 'I didn't know brown people could get freckles!' Another interviewee told me that 'when I started out as a young solicitor, my then supervisor asked me what my first language was at home. Before answering, I asked why he needed to know that. He said he wanted to know how good my English was. I'm born and raised in the UK, graduated from a red brick university with an LLB and got a distinction in my postgraduate studies, and this man wanted to know if my English was good enough!'

Something to note is that many of the women I interviewed here wanted to stay anonymous because they're still working in these places. These examples show us how brown women, despite having been born and raised in the UK, are still being made to prove their worthiness. We still have to prove our Britishness. Still have to verify 'where are you from?'

In her renowned book *Brit(ish)*, writer and activist Afua Hirsch calls it 'The Question' – where are you from? Or should I say, where are you *really* from? She says, 'it can be difficult to communicate to British people who innocently ask The Question, usually out of a harmless, well-meaning curiosity, what is wrong with it [. . .] The more you get asked The Question, the more confused you feel about the answer.' It further 'others' our existence in a space in which we already feel awkward.

I always deliberated over what I should and shouldn't say in response to this question – east London? London? Punjab? Which side of Punjab? Should I go into the story of partition now? Do they even really care? For many minority communities, it's hard to know where 'home' even is anymore. In the words of one of my favourite poets, Ijeoma Umebinyuo, we are 'too foreign for here, too foreign for there. Never enough for both.' For the Punjabi Sikh community, thinking about the question of home, in fact, often brings up deep and traumatic pain. As a marginalized and oppressed group in India who are searching for self-sovereignty, many Punjabi Sikh's may prefer to call themselves Punjabi rather than Indian. Those from Jammu and Kashmir may feel the same. Other marginalized communities, too, might feel this pain. Not welcome 'here' and not welcome or safe 'there'. These are the nuances that are never considered when 'The Question' is asked. If you're feeling as confused as I am, that's OK. Over time I started to displace the importance of giving an adequate answer and instead spent the last few years trying to understand what home really meant to me. Where did I feel at home?

When I was younger, I would hate going back to Punjab during my school holidays. I'd see my friends going on holiday to Disneyland or going skiing in Switzerland, and here I was going to the *pind*. During my teenage years, there was a long period where I didn't go, despite my grandparents going twice a year. Now, as an adult, I go at least once a year. Maybe it's a sense of yearning to find all those little pieces that feel like home. We go back to my babaji's *pind*, and memories of playing in the courtyard with my siblings would come flooding back. Memories of my grandma making me *kheer* and playing with the chickens. Every time I go back, I stare up at that house where our story began, and I feel an ache in the pit of my stomach, an ache that fills me with a sense of both pain and joy that my story has so many beautiful layers and dimensions. But I also feel a sense of home in the streets of London and in the hustle and bustle of the East End. I feel at home in libraries. I feel at home lying on my husband's chest. I feel at home when I sit at my mother's feet, and she rubs coconut oil in my hair. I feel at home when I eat my mother's food. In Susheila Nasta's work *Home Truths: Fictions of the South Asian Diaspora in Britain*, she defines 'home' as a space not necessarily where one belongs, but the place which one starts from. 'Home', 'homely', 'feel at home', 'homesick' – all the terms imply the same meaning, in one way or another, the creation of a 'comfort zone' where one feels absolutely reassured and at ease. I feel at home knowing there is a brown sisterhood, a continuing collective identity that is growing and evolving. Maybe the more at home I feel in that, the less unnerved I'll be when I get asked 'The Question'.

Home can be found in all kinds of places. In the food that we eat, in the music we listen to. In the people that we love. No matter who they are . . . Which brings me on to another nasty microaggression – an underlying, pervasive assumption that brown girls can't be gay. As well as all the other microaggressions we've seen, queer brown women can also be subjected to racially charged forms of discrimination within the LGBTQ+ community. Saima Razzaq, activist and chair of SEEDS (Supporting Education of Equality and Diversity in Schools), told me that she had experienced more sexist and racially charged microaggressions from within the queer community than she has anywhere else. Saima said, 'I'm often told you can't be gay and Muslim by non-Muslims which is the most baffling thing. How can someone who knows nothing about my faith or my lived experience comment on what I can or can't do? It's unfortunate, but a lot of these microaggressions come from cis-gendered white queer males who clearly don't understand their privilege.' It's a double-edged sword. On the one hand, queer brown women are expected to assimilate into a Western idea of their queer identity and then at the same time, deal with the erasure of brown culture within the LGBTQ+ community.[7]

Microaggressions can come from within our communities too. Saying things like, 'you're not like other brown girls', or derogative comments related to that are just as toxic. This self-deprecation, sometimes disguised as humour, derives from internalizing the opinion that we're not good enough. It's one thing receiving these kinds of comments from white people, but it's exhausting to then have them reinforced by our own communities. Vaani Kaur, a teacher and social activist from London, tells me, 'When I get asked what I do for a living, I proudly say "I am a secondary school teacher." It's met with the same response every single time. "Maths or science?" "English actually," I reply, already knowing where the conversation is heading. Inevitably this is followed with a string of uninvited comments about how Indians don't teach English, who would learn that from us and am I sure I don't want to teach maths? But we do teach English, lots of people want to, and I will be sticking to it.'

Back in 2018, I went to see a stunning play called *Spun* by Rabiah Hussain. The play was about two British Pakistani girls from east London, not too far from where I grew up. Her characters, Safa and Aisha, explore themes of friendship and belonging in the wake of the 7/7 terror attacks. The play reveals the microaggressions that Safa experienced when she started working in the city after the girls left university, the struggles of trying to stay connected to one's roots as well as all the everyday nuances of being a brown girl in the UK. In an interview with *Litro* magazine, Rabiah said: 'If you're an Asian girl you're expected to write about honour killings [. . .] If you see South Asian communities on stage there's always something relating to terrorism, or they'll be on the opposite end of the spectrum and have completely let go of their culture and identity.' Despite the play hinging around a terrorist attack, something that she was initially reluctant to include, it's instead centred on how these significant events impacted *our* existence in the white Western world. The play itself was inspired by Rabiah's own personal experience of microaggressions in the world of work. She tells *Litro* magazine that she once received a Christmas present from another Asian colleague and someone joked: 'I hope there's no bomb in there.' I'd never seen a play like this before, one that so intimately explored the many microaggressions that make up the brown experience. I cried pretty much the whole way through. Maybe it's because I felt happy that I wasn't alone in how I felt inside, as a brown woman wanting to uphold and honour her identity, but continuously battling off assumptions, expectations, insecurities and, of course, microaggressions. Maybe it's because it made me feel seen.

## *The art of responding*

Like Rabiah, I was never sure how I should react when I faced these daily microaggressions, except to release them into my writing. Faced with these ignorant comments, I was usually too stunned to generate a witty or snappy comeback at the time, and would usually come up with a wicked one in the shower later that day, thinking, 'Damn it, I should have said that earlier.' Sometimes I would even question whether or not I was actually being insulted. Do you ever wonder, 'Am I being too sensitive'?

Because, trust me, you're not. We need to stop gaslighting ourselves. Repeat after me – 'My feelings are completely valid, and I have the right to express them.' It's OK to feel scared, confused or fully pissed off in these moments. But here are a few things you can do:

*Do nothing.* This could be your initial response. It was mine for a very long time. It might be emotionally draining to have to confront the perpetrator then and there, and that's OK. Protect your energy if you need to. You might not feel safe or comfortable discussing it in that space and time. But I warn you, you might be left wondering what exactly happened and why. And you'll have to depend on yourself for a sense of closure and make peace with the situation, knowing it might happen again.

*Respond back.* Call it out or ask them what they meant by their comment or question. 'What did you mean by that?' Give them a moment to check themselves, but feel free to describe how you interpreted their question. Never laugh it off. A new popular favourite of mine is to say, 'I don't get it', and ask them to explain what they mean. They'll most likely go quiet and squirm. Or you could be witty about it. If someone says, 'Your English is so good,' you could say, 'So is yours!' Hand the micro-aggression back to them and wait. Or you could use this as a time to educate – 'Let's take a minute to unpack what you just said.' Be aware that this approach can be risky. They might make excuses for their behaviour. They may gaslight you. They could get defensive, maybe even hostile towards you, so only use this option if you feel safe and comfortable to. This is where it helps to have some of what Susan Cousins considers 'environmental mastery', as described in her work *Overcoming Everyday Racism*. This 'mastery' is where we learn and develop a range of strategies and responses, first by considering how supportive or unsupportive our environment is. Cousins suggests that a supportive environment would be 'barrier free', 'open-minded', 'inclusive' and 'comforting', as opposed to 'cliquey', 'hostile' and 'critical'. See which of these words relate to your workplace environment more than the others, it may impact which approach you decide to take and when. 'Environmental mastery' also makes you consider whether you have a 'physical buffer zone' – do you have somewhere that Cousins suggests is 'yours'?[8] This could be your desk or somewhere you can go to have a coffee or take a quiet breather when you need to.

*Take some time, respond later.* I fully appreciate that you can't always say something right away. When you've got to put food on the table and have mouths to feed, you may have to think twice about shaking up your place in an establishment. So, take a moment. Breathe. This might give you a chance to assess the situation a little better, put into writing what has been said and explain why the event was offensive. You might want to approach another colleague who you trust to help you deal with the situation or, at the very least, be empathetic. If it can't be a colleague, make sure you do talk to someone about it. As we saw in Chapter 1, bottling in our pain isn't helping anyone. Hopefully, this book will show you that there is a sisterhood out there, waiting to support you. You're not alone in this. You'll realize that those comments you thought were problematic aren't just in your head, they are real and happen to a lot of us. You can't let it slide. Make sure you do expose the situation eventually.

At the end of the day, it is entirely up to you how much investment you make in addressing the microaggressions that you experience. You can respond when you want, how you want.

I wouldn't want you to feel even more pressure around this. Only respond if you feel you're going to be empowered by it. But remember, if you're feeling hurt, anxious or unsafe, don't bottle it in. Speak to someone. Let it out.

## Calling all white allies

Now, for those of you reading this who want to be a better ally to people of colour in the workplace, or anywhere for that matter, here is what you can do. Firstly, become aware of your own biases, preconceptions and fears. Some of these might be unconscious but start checking your behaviours, comments and actions. I know it's uncomfortable to assess your power and privilege but, trust me, it can't be as awkward as being mistaken for the cleaner or being asked if you've read the *Kama Sutra*.

Speak up if you witness any bullshit because sometimes your silence can speak volumes. Don't be a bystander; if someone you know reveals their racist beliefs and you hear any of these microaggressive comments flying around, challenge them. Don't let it slide just because we're not present. And if you're the one perpetuating some of these behaviours, take a moment to reflect. I appreciate that you might not have meant it in a harmful way, but hopefully you now understand how it can cause harm to the recipient.

As white allies, we need you to be less performative and *really* learn to listen and be humble. For example, admit when you're having difficulty with a person's name. The first step to saying someone's name correctly is actually acknowledging that you can't pronounce it. And don't worry if the other person sees you struggling, it's OK if you have to ask for help. Remember, nothing grows in comfort zones. Take on some of the awkward emotional burden from time to time, trust me, you'll grow so much more from it. The emotional tax shouldn't all be on us. Take some time to educate yourself, read up on the history, culture and experiences of other people. Try a shelf-reflection* and if there doesn't seem like a diverse array of authors and books, get some, and read them! That, as well as taking the time to listen, can go a long way in helping you become a better ally.

Once these basic grounds are covered, what we then need to see is not just allyship from white people, but true solidarity and coalition with marginalized or oppressed groups fighting for policy, legislative and institutional change in the workplace. It's only when I recently stepped back and realized that microaggressions are actually just one piece of a systemically problematic machine, that I recognized that we need more than just white people being nice to us. That's a given. We now need you to carry some of the weight that comes with fighting for racial and gender equality. Because we're tired, and we should be able to exist authentically, safely and joyfully in our places of work.

Brown women are by far some of the most resilient women I have ever met, but we can't always be strong. Even after confronting the microaggressions and/or going through the appropriate channels, there will be moments when we still don't get the apology we deserve. And that becomes another painful paper cut that we have to endure. In those moments, remember to always speak to yourself with immense amounts of love and

* [*shelf-reflection*, noun; to reflect on the books on your bookshelf]

compassion. Geena Saini, who is currently working on her doctorate in clinical psychology, told me that someone she worked with made a comment suggesting she only got onto the PhD as a tick-box exercise. 'It was crushing, it made me think about my worth and why I got into becoming a clinical psychologist. I was affected by it for weeks. I spoke to my supervisor about it, and she helped me, as did the support from friends. When the person was called out, they couldn't even remember saying it, so even when given the chance to redeem themselves, they didn't. But I was compassionate towards myself and wrote down and reminded myself why I deserved to be on this course.'

As a woman of colour, the continuous self-checking, self-sufficiency and projection of a strong exterior can get really heavy, so be kind and understanding with yourself. Sometimes, our personality in the workplace isn't always based on our core values but on what we've had to build up as protection because of the situations and circumstances we have been in. We've proven to ourselves that we can be strong, be everything and anything we want to be, but there will be a point where we crave a bit of softness. How can we comfort and care for ourselves in these moments? So, after all those paper cuts, make sure you take time to heal before you put on your cape and take on the world again.

# CHAPTER 4

# SMASHING SHAME

*Menstruation and Other Taboos*

*i would sneak my pads*
*into the house as if they were drugs*
*babies are expected of me*
*but my monthly madness isn't an open conversation*
*keep that behind closed doors*
*or closed legs*
*crossed legs*

*rouge on my jeans,*
*my thighs are blushing like my cheeks*
*because i leaked*
*with the embarrassment*
*ashamed of the stains on my covers*
*as if i committed murder*
*scrubbing the evidence in secret*

*all that we're killing*
*is a young girl's self-worth*
*as long as they can provide a healthy birth*
*right?*

*and now i'll serve my time*
*one week, once a month.*
*a life sentence.*

*blood*

'The blue one, with the wings!' I cried to my husband down the phone. 'Wings? Where is your vagina flying off to?' he cheekily replies. I'm about to perform a spoken word poem in front of thousands of people in Westminster Abbey, including celebrities, politicians and the entire royal family, and my husband chooses this as a time to show off his comedy skills. And, I must add, it was going to be broadcast live on the BBC across the world. I was unprepared and unpadded and my period had started. I was pretty sure that the last thing 'Lilibet' wanted to see was a period stain showing through my dress. It would have been quite the political statement, though . . . but I digress. My hubby, Mr Indy Hothi, managed to get back in time for me to pad up just before I went on to perform. The performance went well and I managed not to fall flat on my face – win! No one would have known I was bleeding heavily throughout. I tried to tell my mum about my period fiasco after the performance, but she was more excited by the fact that she got to sit next to Ainsley Harriott. She was also sitting near One Direction's Liam Payne, which I personally would have been more excited about, but Mum was more enthusiastic about the new recipes she'd picked up from Ainsley.

My husband, as well as the other men in my life, is now pretty used to hearing me speak about my periods, which pads I need and everything else that comes with the joys and pains of menstruating every month. But that wasn't always the case. Let's rewind to the summer when I had just turned thirteen, and I found the first little red droplets in my knickers. I was scared and confused and called for my mum, who was downstairs in the kitchen. Mum snuck me a pad under the door, whispered in a hushed voice that I should remove the backing to the pad and stick it on my knickers (and not the other way round!) and that was that. No follow-up conversations and definitely no celebrations. It was all pretty anticlimactic, to be honest. But the hushed transfers of pads continued throughout my teenage years. We would come back from the pharmacy, and I would run upstairs quickly with the bag and put it in my room before anyone – specifically the men of the house – saw. I would have to wrap it up in layers of tissue and then a plastic bag before putting it in any bin, just in case anyone opened the bin and, God forbid, saw it.

My only understanding of periods before this point had come from school when in Year 6, all the girls were asked to go to the hall for a 'special assembly'. I remember all the boys got to go out and play in the playground, and I, of course, was super jealous. It felt like a punishment. I would soon learn this was one of the many 'punishments' I would have to endure, simply for being a girl. The special assembly for us Year 6 girls consisted of an old school cassette being played on a 28in TV which included a few diagrams, a brief explanation about puberty from the school nurse and a goody bag with pads to leave with. The only follow-up from that was a few biology lessons in early secondary school, where I remember being shown where your body hair will grow and how not to get pregnant. Fast forward to the present day, and the situation in schools isn't looking too different. Add a layer of shame, a dash of discomfort and a splash of stigma from your brown household and there you have it, the journey of menstruation for most brown girls. I know brown women who have changed their wedding date because of their periods. I know brown women who have never used tampons in case it impacted their 'virginity'. I know brown women who have even felt the need to hide their used pads from their in-laws and throw them away on their way to work.

From the outset, my periods had been spotty. I would have a consistent cycle for a few months, they were heavy and painful, but they came, and then nothing for a while. But it was when I was around fifteen that I started spotting continuously . . . For six months . . . And I didn't tell anyone. Imagine, I was wearing pads for six months, and allowed myself to suffer in silence all that time because I was never encouraged to talk about them. It was due to polycystic ovary syndrome (PCOS), a condition that affects one in every ten women in the UK. My 182 days of bleeding taught me one thing. Like most of the other emotional and physical pain brown women endure in their lifetime, my period would be no exception. I would soon learn that this silence about periods, especially concerning my pain and discomfort, would force me to endure debilitating health problems. As brown women, we ignore the vital signs of underlying health issues because we have been taught to shun and shame them. I would have been one of the 80 per cent of adolescent girls in the UK who experience concerning menstrual symptoms.[1]

After the six months of bleeding, my body felt drained. My anaemia* was getting worse, I felt exhausted all the time, and it

---

* Menstruation in healthy women does not automatically cause iron deficiency anaemia. Blood loss during a period in healthy women is not more than 80ml (around 3 tablespoons). My blood loss was more severe.

was something my family picked up on. We eventually went to the doctor when I was around sixteen, and that's when I first confessed to my continuous bleeding. I say 'confessed' because at the time, it did feel like I and my body were doing something wrong, and I was ready for the punishment. The doctor sent me away for a few blood tests and scans, and there it was, PCOS. 'Despite its name, PCOS doesn't actually mean you have cysts on your ovaries. It actually means your ovaries become enlarged and contain fluid-filled sacs called follicles,' the GP told me. I looked at her blankly . . . She might as well have been speaking in code because I had no idea what she was telling me . . . 'So, when do you plan on having children?' she asked next. And there we have it. At the age of sixteen, I was already forced to worry that I might find it hard to conceive in the future, when the only thing I should have been worrying about was whether or not I was going to finish my English coursework on time. She put me on the pill, told me to do some research online and come back to see her in six months. And that was it. My Google research didn't help with my confusion, either. 'The exact cause of PCOS is unknown, but it often runs in families,' the NHS website told me. Fast forward to the present day, and that's still what it says.

It made me empathize with the pre-Google generation, women like my mum or grandma, who would have had even fewer resources to go to when they were stuck for information about what was happening to their bodies.

### Shame on who?

The interesting thing about menstruation is that it doesn't matter where you are in the world, East, West, North or South;

it doesn't matter what culture you belong to or how 'modern' or forward-thinking the society sees itself, there is still a massive stigma attached to menstruation. Periods are still a taboo for most societies. Gabrielle Jackson, author of *Pain and Prejudice: A call to arms for women and their bodies*, focused her work on Australia, Jennifer Weiss-Wolf wrote about the menstrual situation in the USA in her work *Periods Gone Public*, and Emma Barnett recently covered the UK context in her book *Period*. But much of the menstruation conversation is still dominated by white voices, so it's vital that we brown women add a little masala to the mix.

It's important to recognize that not all women experience menstruation in the same way. Different cultures and religions view and manage their menstruation very differently. In Islam, menstruating women, *haa'idh*, should not touch the Quran or enter a mosque, and there are prohibitions around physical intimacy. They are also encouraged not to fast if they're on their period during Ramadan, for the benefit of the women, who would probably not want to go without food during their period.[2] Hindu women are often encouraged not to enter temples, prepare or touch food during this time, but not always. Sikh women are free to meditate and pray, visit the Gurdwara, and partake in *sewa*, selfless service.[3] But whether that is widely accepted by the community is another question. I guess what's important to acknowledge when we talk about views on the 'purity' and 'impurity' of menstruation in faith is that we always see the really negative stories. Later in the chapter, we will see how women have interpreted these teachings in different ways, ways in which they are also empowered.

The global picture is pretty bleak. The charity WaterAid

found that in Sri Lanka, 66 per cent of girls reported not receiving any information about menstruation before the first time they started their period. More than one-third of girls in the region miss school days during their period; 31 per cent of girls in Bangladesh said menstruation affects their attendance and this rose to about 37 per cent in Afghanistan and Sri Lanka.[4] In India, around 52 per cent of girls don't get any information about their periods. In India's Tamil Nadu state, a twelve-year-old took her own life after a teacher embarrassed her in front of the whole class when she bled through her uniform. After jumping off a building near her home, she was found dead, leaving a note saying her teacher had 'tortured her'. The *chhaupdi* huts in Nepal made headlines when it was found that almost 19 per cent of women are banished to the huts during their time of the month.[5] This antiquated belief is that they need to be isolated because their period may bring bad luck on the family, crops and livestock. Despite it being outlawed by the Supreme Court in 2005, to be upheld, a formal complaint must be filed against the family members, which is pretty unlikely.

Such restrictions around what women can and can't do during their periods came to a head in 2018, when a Supreme Court of India ruling ended a ban on women of menstruating age from entering the Sabarimala temple in Kerala. The local government supported the ban, but many Hindus demonstrated against this state interference in religion. This, in turn, incited counter-demonstrations by women who favoured the ruling. In January 2019, Bindu Ammini became the face of the demonstrations, as she was the first woman of menstruating age to enter the Sabarimala temple. When I spoke to activist, writer and speaker Sangeeta Pillai, the founder of Soul Sutras and the award-winning *Masala Podcast*, she had a personal story about Sabarimala from her childhood. She told me, 'I started my first period at the age of twelve. It was around the same time that my dad decided to go to Sabarimala. This meant that little old menstruating me had to be kept away from her father, as he had to stay pure in body and mind for the forty-one days that he was fasting. I wasn't even allowed to accidentally brush past him.' To navigate these situations as a child must have been tough. The recent Sabarimala protests shifted the menstruation narrative worldwide. As the buzz around Sabarimala increased on social media, women began to take advantage of the opportunity to start conversations in the public sphere here in the UK, specifically relating to discussions surrounding menstrual taboos and access to menstrual products.

It became apparent that these concerns span different cultures and countries. We shouldn't be mistaken of thinking this is a faraway issue. It's happening on our turf too. A recent study by Plan International UK reported that 1 in 10 girls aged fourteen to twenty-one can't afford menstrual products on a regular basis, forcing some to stay home from school, and 42 per cent have resorted to using makeshift period ware such as paper and socks.[6] In addition to that, according to a survey by Public Health England in 2018, menstrual issues were reported by half of the women in all age groups and three-quarters of sixteen- to twenty-four-year-olds.[7] So if it's impacting so many of us, why is there so little known about how to manage our periods and why is it still so stigmatized? The impurity complex is where the story begins, but where does it end? How can we encourage people to see that our periods aren't a waste disposal system, and we aren't getting rid of 'dirty blood'? Because our bodies aren't polluted.

One way we can go about changing this is considering the language and terminology that we use. I remember when I first became an ambassador for Binti International, an amazing charity on a mission to provide menstrual dignity to all girls worldwide. The founder and now my good friend, Manjit Gill, told me they no longer use the word sanitary towels. 'Sanitary makes our periods sound like they're dirty, so we don't use that word anymore. Instead, we say menstrual products,' she told me. I was mind-blown. They may just seem like subtle euphemisms, but by using words like sanitary and hygiene, we're continually reinforcing the taboos we're trying so hard to break.

Try not to forget that multinational companies usually use this kind of language, using *their* language to talk about our bodies. Even Menstrual 'Hygiene' Day, which takes place on 28 May every year, is a little problematic. Maybe we should go for Menstrual Health Day instead? In Nadiya Hussain's memoir, *Finding My Voice*, she recalls being at her grandmother's house when her period started. Her nan encouraged Nadiya to call her mum, and she said down the phone that 'My illness has started.'[8] Rather than stating what it was – a period – she had to use the word illness instead. Think about the words and euphemisms that you've used over the years with your friends and family, rather than using the word period, because according to International Women's Health Coalition there are 5,000 of them!

## *Medical men and brown bodies*

The lack of research into women's health, specifically concerning our menstruation, is pretty damning. This is even more of an issue for women of colour. Brown women have been let down by unequal and archaic approaches to female health for decades. Much of the research out there still falls back on stereotypical narratives, such as that brown women are more vulnerable, because of outdated assumptions like lack of language skills. This might have been an excuse three decades ago, but it's not anymore. This shows us that even in medical research, the white body, specifically the white male cis body, is more of a priority. It's seen as the default. Gabrielle Jackson notes in her work that 'women's pain is all too often dismissed, their illnesses misdiagnosed or ignored [. . .] In medicine, man is the default human being. Any deviation is atypical, abnormal, deficient.'[9] This has often been referred to as the Yentl Syndrome.[10]

The statistics that we *do* have on brown women's health are often harrowing. According to the 2019 Mothers and Babies Reducing Risk through Audit and Confidential Enquiries (MBRRACE) Report, Black and Asian women have a higher risk of dying in pregnancy compared to white women, with Black women four times as likely and Asian women twice as likely.[11] It was also found that Asian new-born babies are 60 per cent more likely to die than white babies. The situation became even more sinister when I learnt that the publication of the report was halted under 'electoral purdah' during the December 2019 election period, which is 'the ban on civil servants publishing politically sensitive information during an election period'. It appears they were attempting to hide the findings of the report in the hope that it wouldn't sway voters. This event, and the overall lack of research into brown women's health, raises a lot of questions to which there are still no clear answers. It just goes to show that the lives and health of brown and black women have not been, and will not be a priority for those at the top.

You may have seen quotes saying periods can be as painful as a heart attack. Gynaecologist Dr Jen Gunter suggests that they are even *more* painful than a heart attack. She suggests that a more accurate analogy would be childbirth or cutting your finger off without an anaesthetic. However, painful periods, also known as dysmenorrhoea, have still had very little research and understanding due to lack of funding. That's probably because funding panels are – you guessed it – male-dominated and mostly white. Thus, until more research goes into why periods can be so painful for some of us and how to deal with it, we've got to endure pain that's similar to cutting off our fingers each month. Nice.

There is also inadequate research into what benefits or long-term impact medical approaches like the pill might have on our bodies. A lot of the research is centred around contraceptive use, specifically for South Asian married women, but very little health-based approaches.[12] For those of us who have been on the combined pill, you may recall being told to take a break for one week a month to have your withdrawal bleed, to mimic a monthly period. The Faculty of Sexual and Reproductive Healthcare (FSRH) updated their guidelines in January 2019 to state that there were actually no health benefits to the 'fake period'. Some have even suggested that this was implemented to make the pill more acceptable to the Catholic Church, as it would seem more natural to bleed a few days a month.

Neelam Heera, founder of Cysters, a charity tackling the misconceptions around reproductive health, also highlighted that 'it is predominantly white researchers that contact communities of colour. The lack of trust or connection makes it difficult.' She also noted that when data is collected, 'the information found hardly ever disseminates back into the community again.' Cysters is working hard to fill that gap. 'Cysters have been connecting communities with researchers, acting as the conjugate between them,' Neelam tells me.

I also found very limited literature on brown folk who may be gender-non-conforming or don't identify as women but still menstruate. Many people who do not identify as women have female sex organs. In a blog post for Cysters, Manpreet told readers that 'When I was 20 years old, I came out as a transgender man. Since then, I started having periods as a man. I began to notice the accessibility issues immediately, especially when I would use public bathrooms.' The trans experience and the non-binary folk have all been completely ignored in clinical research to do with menstruation, and the application of an intersectional lens that also considers race seems like it'll be years away. Manpreet put it beautifully, 'A uterus can belong to anybody, so it becomes crucial to do work that is inclusive.'

Although we've seen period taboos being tackled through social media campaigns, as we can see, this has yet to permeate the medical discourse. There is still hardly any research on pain prevention or pain relief and on devices such as tampons, menstrual cups and pads. I always do wonder, if it were men that were suffering from the pain, would research have been funded decades ago?

### Talk dirty to me

So, until there is more medical research on our periods, I guess it's up to us as a community to start talking about it more ourselves, right? But how do we do that when periods are still deemed as a dirty, almost naughty thing to talk about? I say naughty because it's clear that the period is another part of the brown woman's body that has been overly sexualized. What I mean by this is that for most brown women and men, periods are purely associated with fertility and having babies, which is associated with having sex to make the baby, which, of course, is too taboo to talk about. Neelam even told me that when she would speak about the work of Cysters online, 'Men, specifically South Asian men, would respond back with profanity, using it as an opportunity to treat me like I'm being sexually promiscuous!' As a result, both public and private spheres continue to sexualize menstruation, so it remains a topic that still can't be spoken about openly, regardless of gender. It's only appropriate amongst the whispers of women behind closed doors (or in my case with my mum, through closed doors). It's this same sexualization of our bodies that tells us to pull up our top (because our cleavage has been sexualized) or to tie back our hair (because the hair on our head has been sexualized) or hide our bra strap (because the bra strap means we have boobies!). And this starts so early in a woman's life: we've been sexualizing girls' bodies from as young as the age of eleven, or whenever they get their first period. And it's not fair.

Tasnia Shahjahan wrote in *Brown Girl Magazine* that 'as an unmarried Bangladeshi-Muslim woman, the fact that I take birth control pills is an eyebrow-raising concern for many people in my own community. Even though one might argue that the choices I make about my body should be solely my own concern, this often is not the case in family-oriented communities.' Here we can see that even the pill has been sexualized. Many people automatically assume that using the pill is an indication of sexual activity, rather than considering that it may be being used as medication to manage heavy, painful or irregular bleeding. I say bleeding intentionally because it's not really the blood our community has a problem with. I know a lot of guys, and girls for that matter, who can watch *The Texas Chainsaw Massacre* without squirming. It's the fact that the blood is coming out of a woman's body. It's also important to note that for some people (and by people I mean men), periods, like public breastfeeding, remind them of the uncomfortable truth that our body is not just an object of sexual desire. Therefore, it becomes easier for people to frame periods as something necessary for fertility, or it's easier to consider them dirty and just not talk about them at all. If instead, periods were seen as a normal bodily process, just like other functions of the body, and if we moved away from the idea that our periods are associated with the sexual parts of our bodies, maybe we could finally desexualize and destigmatize the subject. That way, we can talk about them more openly and normally.

Normalizing our discussions around periods will not only benefit the health and happiness of the brown girls in our communities but will have wider positive impacts as well. Innovations like reusable period underwear, menstrual cups and cycle-tracking apps have all come out of a new generation of women who refuse to stay hushed about their period. Not only are these products good for women's overall health, they are also working to tackle period poverty and helping low-income communities across the world. A great example is LUÜNA Naturals. For every menstrual cup sold, it donates one, as well as providing education, to vulnerable communities. These innovations also tackle the period plastic pollution. According to the Women's Environment

Network (WEN), the average woman uses 11,000 disposable menstrual products over thirty years. Knowing that all the pads I have ever used are lying in a landfill somewhere, taking around a thousand years to biodegrade, made me feel pretty crappy, so I've been using reusable pads for over two years now. Speaking of the WEN, they recently began a digital series entitled #PlasticFree-PeriodsReframed to highlight the incredible women of colour spearheading the plastic-free periods movement. So often the movement gets hijacked by wealthy and/or white women, so the need to 'centre and celebrate Black and Peoples of Colour in this space who are owning the narrative on sustainable periods', as WEN emphasizes, is incredibly vital.

## *Periods in the political playground*

Maybe this shows us that things are finally moving and shaking in the right direction, albeit slowly. Our periods have now entered the political playground, and we've turned up with the best new games, with discussions around how it should be taught, tackling stigma and access inequality. On Menstrual Hygiene Day in 2019, the then Minister for Women and Equalities in the UK, Penny Mordaunt, announced the government's new Period Poverty Taskforce, co-chaired by Plan International UK, Procter & Gamble and herself. The taskforce (I love that it sounds like a new kind of *Avengers*) included Bloody Good Period, phs Group, Irise International, London School of Hygiene & Tropical Medicine, Sport England, and two other vital contributors, PSHE Association to provide a school focus and Binti International – yay! I got to attend the meeting on behalf of Binti and was so excited by all the potential ideas floating about in that room, some of which have come to life. I witnessed what I would like to call the period revolution in action, or what some have coined the 'period crusade'. Not sure if 'crusade' is the best choice of phrasing, but it is equally bloody. There is a history joke somewhere in the last sentence, forgive me. The following year, on 20 January, schools and colleges across the UK were able to access a period product scheme that would provide free period products to all learners. I cried when the news came out. That might sound dramatic to some, but let me tell you why.

I will never forget a few years ago, when I was teaching, and a student of mine stormed out of the classroom, sobbing. Aisha* was an exceptional history student – she loved analysing and evaluating sources, would go above and beyond with her home-work and was always on time for every lesson. So her behaviour that day seemed completely out of character. Another teacher sat in with my class as I went to look for her, and I eventually found her, sobbing at the bottom of the staircase. 'Is everything OK? My lessons aren't that bad, are they?' I jested. A grin appeared from under the tears. She then told me her period had started . . . for the first time. She went on to tell me that she wouldn't be able to buy any pads or ask anyone at home for them. Money was tight at home, her mum and dad were on the verge of sep-arating, and as the eldest sibling with three younger brothers she didn't want to add any extra 'burden' on the family. 'There's no one I can tell in my family, all my cousins are boys, and I've never heard my mum talk about it either.' I was about to start crying with her. My heart sank. 'The pads are £1 in reception,

* Name has been changed.

and I already used my lunch money.' Extortionate, I thought . . . 'I don't want to ask any of the girls in class because they're all going to laugh at me for starting mine so late,' she told me. By 'late' Aisha meant that she started her period in Year 9 whilst many of the other girls had started theirs already. FYI, girls, this isn't late, the average is around age twelve, and she was only a few months older.

At lunchtime, I popped down to the shops and bought her a month's supply. I also checked in with her in the months to come. Maybe I did this because I empathized with that moment of desperation when you need a pad, bad! There was one time at school, when I was on my never-ending period and needed to change my pad, and it was just before a PE lesson was about to start. I disposed of the old one and searched my bag frantically for a new one. Nothing. I called to see if there were any other girls in the toilets. Silence. So, I did what we've all done. I made a makeshift pad out of toilet paper, popped it in place and ran to catch up with the rest of the class. It was one of my favourite PE lessons, trampolining! But then my worst nightmare unfolded. Whilst perfecting my seat jump, I felt the makeshift tissue-pad slide out of the side of my knickers, float down the leg of my tracksuit bottoms and land on the trampoline. There it was – lying in front of me like evidence left at a crime scene! I panicked. I managed to quickly execute a Chun-Li style cartwheel, grabbed the incriminating evidence and legged it out of the gym. If a programme like the period product scheme had existed back then for me when I was in school, and then for Aisha, imagine how much pain it would have saved us both. The scheme, backed by the phs Group, allows schools to order at any point in the year regular pads and tampons and environmentally friendly pads and menstrual cups! This, as we have seen, is good news for all girls, but it is especially good news for brown girls like me and Aisha, who may have more complex issues going on in the background.

## Relearning our bodies

Following on from this good news, from September 2020, teaching both girls *and* boys about periods and menstrual wellbeing became compulsory in all state-funded schools in England (primary and secondary) in PSHE.

Now, for my brown sisters and mummies and perhaps grandmummies, who are way past high school PSHE lessons, your learning is just as important. What self-education are my grown women doing? What teaching is going on in our homes? Is it another awkward dinner table conversation you need to add to your menu? When we've been telling our daughters to lie and sneak and hide when it comes to their periods, what are we *really* teaching them about their bodies, in addition to teaching them that it's OK to lie? And are we getting brown men in on the conversation too? They may not be the ones bleeding, but how is that an excuse? Since when was it OK to not bother educating yourself about something that doesn't affect you personally? If we all lived with that little empathy, we'd all be doomed. Seventeen-year-old Tharnika Kamsanathan, a mentee from The Girls' Network, told me that the day after she started her period, she and her family 'held a small puberty ceremony, which is something most Sri Lankan girls experience.' The Samathi Veedu ceremony, sometimes known as Manjal Neerattu Vizha, is a Sri Lankan and Tamil tradition celebrating a girl's transition into womanhood. Similar traditions can be found in Japanese, Korean, Mayan and Jewish cultures too. However, Sinthuya Veerasingam, a fellow mentee, did tell me that the celebration used to 'inform people a girl has come of age' and was ready for potential suitors, but she suggested that this has changed. Sinthuya said that now 'some people have these celebrations to show off their wealth, whilst some genuinely just want to have a happy celebration with loved ones.'

Self-education matters. The Eve Appeal found that 44 per cent of women couldn't correctly identify a vagina in a diagram. More worryingly, they also found that 15 per cent of women wouldn't go to see their doctor if they found a lump in their vagina. The point is, if we knew our bodies better, perhaps we would live happier and healthier lives. It could even save lives. I know that brown women are used to putting up with pain and putting other people's feelings and thoughts first. It seems to be ingrained in our psyche. But you are never too busy to go to the doctor! You aren't wasting anyone's time! So please, if something doesn't seem right or feel right, ask for help. Pain isn't synonymous with being a woman, so we should stop acting like it is.

Dr Tayyaba Ahmed, a Board Certified Doctor of Physical Medicine and Rehabilitation, told *Brown Girl Magazine* that 'some parents would accuse their daughter of being lazy and trying to get out of doing work and the unfortunate part of this is that so much endometriosis likely went undiagnosed. The fact is 1 in 10 women has endometriosis, and 30 to 40 per cent of women with endometriosis are infertile. [. . .] I wonder if brown parents would encourage the conversation of pelvic pain if they knew that this could affect their daughter's fertility.'

I know these conversations may be difficult to start when

we've got centuries-worth of stigma to smash through, often reinforced with cultural or faith-related expectations. But the faith perspectives may be more positive than we think. Take, for example, Henna Patel's description of Ayurveda when she wrote for *Burnt Roti* magazine: 'Hindus believe in Ayurveda, energy flows and chakras [. . .] It is believed that when we bleed, we are ridding our bodies of all the unnecessary energy that we accumulate from our body getting itself ready for a possible pregnancy. All of this energy is released downward out and away from the body during menstruation. When this downward flow of energy meets other energies, they collide and can cause discomfort in menstruation and generally, an unbalanced mind and body.' She questioned why menstruation hasn't been taught this way to her before: '. . . we've been conditioned into believing that women's menstrual blood is dirty, impure. When, in fact, it is believed that menstruation is a normal and natural energy flow.' This description made me optimistic about the possibility of having a much deeper understanding and connection with our own bodies.

As I mentioned earlier in the chapter, menstruating Muslim women do not fast during Ramadan so that they're able to nourish their bodies when needed and are encouraged to make up for the missed days of fasting when they can. But they shouldn't be made to feel uncomfortable for it. In writer and spoken word artist Hanan Issa's blog post for the *Tribune*, she begins with, 'We've all been there, ladies. Don't deny it. Who hasn't taken a surreptitious look around before scoffing a bite of (insert chosen food here) while on your period in Ramadan?' She goes on to say, 'why do we ladies [. . .] put ourselves through the extra hardship of hiding our Allah-given right to eat when others fast?' Nura Maznavi, writer and co-editor of *Love, InshAllah: The Secret Love Lives of American Muslim Women*, wrote in a post for *Beacon Broadside* that when she overcame the stigma of not fasting during Ramadan because of her period, she was able to experience Ramadan in beautiful new ways. 'I woke up for suhoor each morning with my husband, attended tarawih prayers, increased my Quran recitation, and hosted friends for iftar. Although I wasn't fasting, I still felt the Ramadan spirit. [. . .] This Ramadan, it's time to show myself mercy and let go of the guilt. Instead, I'll focus my energy on creating a home where my daughter grows up to love Ramadan as much as I do . . .' Nura's story shows us so eloquently that even though you might not be able to fast, it doesn't mean you can't get closer to God – if that is what you wish.

When I spoke with Kajal Verma, a student from Brunel University, she told me that because she was menstruating, 'I was told that I wasn't able to attend my own grandad's funeral. Family members tried to convince me it wasn't the "done thing" for Hindu girls. The sad thing was, I knew that he would never think that way, he would have wanted me to be there whether I was on my period or not. So, I still went for him.'

I wanted to share these specific stories, rather than just the negative ones, because I don't want women to internalize the notions of shame that some interpretations of religious ideals might propagate. We should have the autonomy to do whatever we want to do. Pray, don't pray. Go to the temple, don't go to the temple. In other words, do what you want to do, and make sure shame isn't the driver of your decisions. And like Henna Patel, perhaps use it as a chance to understand your body better.

*

Admittedly it was only recently, in my mid-twenties, that I really got to know my body and started my own self-education. I started using an app to track my cycle; it helped me understand when my period would be due, and when I would be ovulating. The app requires you to take your temperature every morning as soon as you wake up, to monitor your cervical mucus and upload the data. You can track these recordings with good old-fashioned pen and paper. I learnt how my temperature fluctuates during the different phases of my cycle, when my body is experiencing an increase either in oestrogen or progesterone and follicle-stimulating hormones. Who knew your temperature readings would teach you so much! It made sense why I would feel more tired during particular times of the month, so I learnt to be gentler with myself on those days. At certain times of my cycle, I realized that I was more likely to get constipated (too much?), so I would nourish myself with more fruit. I learnt that my nipples get super sensitive when I'm ovulating (way too much?) and that the migraines I used to get two days before my period were due to the hormone changes. Sometimes I regret that I didn't get to know my body earlier, purely because it feels like a friend I could have made sooner. It was a friend I could have loved sooner. She should have technically been my first friend! And it was only on reflection that I realized that I found my love for my new friend, my body, through the work of other brown women.

This new friendship with my body began in 2015, in what Jennifer Weiss-Wolf calls 'The Year of the Period'. On 23 March of that year, now a world-renowned poet, Rupi Kaur, posted a photograph of herself on Instagram. The image was of her lying on a bed in her joggers, with a tell-tale stain of blood in-between her legs, and another small droplet on the bed. The images were staged as part of a project for her visual rhetoric course at university, with the help of her sister, Prabh. The photo was taken down by Instagram for 'going against community guidelines', and Rupi rightfully challenged Instagram and reposted it. Instagram later apologized to Rupi and said it had removed it by mistake. Arguably, the incident helped launch her work *Milk and Honey*, which was initially self-published in November 2014 and went on to become a worldwide bestseller.

A month later, another woman helped sow the seeds of my personal period revolution. Musician and Harvard graduate Kiran Gandhi ran the London Marathon with her period free-flowing. Just as she was about to start the race, her period started, and so she made the choice that rather than wear a pad or tampon that would most likely chafe (and who needs that on a 26-mile run?), she would allow herself to free bleed. Kiran used the publicity to highlight the fact that she had made the choice to free bleed that time, but many women around the world don't have that luxury. In her talk at the Women Deliver 2016 Global Conference, Kiran said, 'Stigma is one of the most effective forms of oppression. Why? Because it denies us the vocabulary to talk comfortably and confidently about our own bodies.' On a side note, Kiran is one of the best drummers I have ever heard; she's drummed for the likes of M.I.A. Goals! So two of the most significant political protests concerning periods in 2015, whether intentional or not, were both started by brown women. Let's take a moment just to appreciate that.

Since then, I've been keeping up with the work of women of colour in the menstruation space. Women like Juspreet Kaur, also known as Kaur Health, and Lisa Hendrickson-Jack, author of *The Fifth Vital Sign* have taught me that understanding my menstrual cycle is just as important as understanding my heart rate and blood pressure. Another young brown woman making waves in this period revolution is Amika George. At the age of seventeen, back in April 2017, Amika founded the #FreePeriods organization, spearheading a petition in conjunction with the Red Box Project and The Pink Protest. It was addressed to Westminster with over 200,000 signatories demanding that girls on free school meals should receive free menstrual products. Since then, Amika's accolades have been growing, being named one of *Time*'s Most Influential Teens of 2018, *Teen Vogue* 21 under 21 (for which she was nominated by Emma Watson) and the *Big Issue* Top 100 Changemakers. She has now published a book entitled *Make it Happen* on how to be an activist, reminding us all that we can create big changes in our communities at any age. Hopefully, Amika's story, as well as the work of many other brown women in the period revolution, shows you that there are a lot of positive changes happening out there. Brown women are building a new culture of openness with a generation keen to verbalize the realities of the female experience, putting their comfort, health and autonomy first.

Learning everything we can about our own brown bodies is the first step in empowering ourselves in order to fight for our rightful place in society. With that knowledge, we can continue to fight for brown bodies to be prioritized in activist spaces, in research, in education and in policymaking too. Understand your body and your period. It will provide you with an indescribably universal understanding and camaraderie with all women: even as strangers, we all dig through our handbags for one another when a woman needs a pad or tampon in a public bathroom. We empathize with each other. This compassion is what binds us women together. And it is this universal under-standing, if used to challenge stigma and shame, that might just change the world. Remember, it only takes one generation to change the status quo.

When, and if, I have kids someday, a boy or girl, I want them to be able to talk about periods openly. To never have to hide their pads (environmentally friendly ones, of course). We will ensure that giving birth and becoming a mother are not seen as the only important aspects of talking about menstruation. We shall say the word period in my house. We shall voice our pain and discomfort. We will not have to suffer in silence. We will celebrate them. We will understand them. After all, where would we all bloody be without them?

# CHAPTER 5

# RIPPED ROOTS

*Brown Bodies, Body Hair and Colourism*

*since when did 'woman' become a hairless word?*
*because i'm pretty sure that even eve had*
*some fur under her sleeve*
*i mean*
*the hypocrisy is that the hair out of my*
*head makes me feminine*
*but anything below my eyebrows makes me*
*some ape-like specimen*
*so, we remove that hair*
*trimming ourselves into someone sexier*
*but maybe i'm reading this all wrong like*
*i've got dyslexia*
*because when i read 'woman'*
*i don't read a hairless word.*

**a hairless word**

At the age of nine, I decided to use my dad's old razor to shave my legs before a friend's birthday party. I cut myself so deeply near the dip of my ankle that I still have the scar today. I remember my sister had laid out a beautiful green dungaree dress for me to wear. She had bought it for me a few weeks earlier, on my birthday, but I was so embarrassed to show anyone my bleeding (and still hairy) leg that I told her I hated the dress and wanted to wear something else instead. I'm sorry, Sis.

At the age of eleven, I used my mum's Jolen Cream Bleach on my sideburns because the boy I sat next to in class told me I looked like a gorilla . . . It gave me a rash that lasted for the next seven days. At fourteen, I attempted to use hot wax to remove my upper lip hair . . . I must have overheated the wax in the microwave and consequently burnt the soft, tender skin right off. The result: I looked like I had an even darker moustache – Sod's Law. At sixteen, I plucked away at the unibrow that sat neatly on the bridge of my nose like the wings of a bat. The plucking continued to the east and west of the unibrow until I was left with two unrecognizably matchstick-thin eyebrows. At eighteen, I used Nair hair removal cream on my underarm hair. I must have left it on for too long because it started stinging like crazy and I couldn't put deodorant on for weeks. Finally, in my early twenties, I saved up enough money for laser hair removal, thinking it would be the permanent solution to rid myself of something I detested so much. But nothing was permanent except for the hate I seemed to have developed for my own body.

These little horror stories will sound familiar to most women. But it's worse for most brown women – our body hair is thick and dark like the roots of a sycamore. Our body hair follicles are thick by genetic design, which often means they will not go down without a fight. I say body hair specifically because it's anything below the eyebrows that we seem to have a problem with. And as we can see from my experiences, this association with 'pain is beauty and beauty is pain' starts very young, fuelled by the desire for smooth-sleek-hairless-skin like the skin in all the adverts. Am I the only one who couldn't understand why they were always shaving already hairless skin? We have to try twice as hard to keep up with the Joneses – or should I say Kardashians (who I assume, because of their Armenian descent, would be equally as hairy). Danisha Kaur, a recent graduate in Ancient History and Archaeology from the University of Birmingham, notes in an article for *Asian Woman Festival* that 'growing up in a predominantly Caucasian society, surrounded by women who have light hair (a sort of blonde fuzz) that appears to be practically imperceptible, it became clear that they would never go through the same struggles and insecurities that I would go through as an Asian woman.' Spot on, Danisha!

Why is it that we have added this excessive labour to our lives? A labour that forces us to perform a full-body exorcism every time we're in the shower? We've all been there, applying shaving cream all over our bodies so we end up looking like the abominable snowman,* right? We're not alone. In her famous work *The Beauty Myth*, Naomi Wolf argues that this is a part of the 'Third Shift'. This is the labour shift we perform in addition to our paid job and domestic work. She writes: 'women have more money and power and scope and legal recognition than we have ever had before; but in terms of how we feel about ourselves physically, we may actually be worse off than our unliberated grandmothers.' I agree with Naomi here, that we probably feel worse about our brown bodies, in terms of self-esteem, than previous generations did. We're surrounded by social media and advertisements displaying white, hairless, sleek, flawless and pore-less skin, close up and from every angle. We're encouraged to perform this expensive, repetitive and invisible labour time and time again to meet the feminine ideal. Hairlessness is not synonymous with the female body. It requires work . . . As if we don't have enough on our shoulders already.

## A very hairy subject

In her article 'Politics of Hair Removal', writer and budding lawyer Duriba Khan points out that body hair, specifically on South Asian women, has been ignored in conversations concerning third-wave feminism. She argues that 'we have no one to blame for this but ourselves.' Is she right? Have we been hiding how we feel in our brown bodies for too long, in an effort to reach the standards of the white body we have put up on a pedestal? I thought that seeing celebrities like Madonna, Britney

---

* [*abominable snowman*, noun; a creature covered in shaving foam, usually found in the shower]

and Miley Cyrus exposing their armpit hair over the years would have made me feel empowered and – dare I say – cute. But it didn't. And I couldn't help wondering why. Maybe it was because their faint layer of blonde or light brown hair was privileged enough to find its way on to porcelain pits. Perhaps it was because it was another area of feminism that women of colour had been excluded from. As Aisha Salim, a mental health social worker from east London, so perfectly put it in an interview with *Huffington Post*, 'When a white woman embraces her armpit hair, it's revolutionary. When a woman of colour does it, it's more grotesque. Many women of colour that I know, as well as myself, are not in a position where we feel like we have the choice to be embracing armpit hair.' Or maybe it was the sneers and giggles from the white girls in my swimming class at age nine that taught me that my brown body was something I should be ashamed of. Whilst some of them would pull off their clothes without a care in the world, I would go and get changed in a toilet cubicle, staring down at what I thought were the 'abnormalities' of my own body.

Why is it that we became so obsessed with hairless bodies? What ignited this disgust for body hair? And why is it that it's only body hair on women that people seem to have a problem with? Is it just another tool of patriarchal control over women's bodies? I know some people might be reading this and thinking, 'Chill, Jaspreet, it's my body, and it's my choice to remove my body hair because I want to.' And yes, of course it is, and power to you for thinking that way. But I just want to assess what brought you to that 'choice'. By asking these questions about the taboo that is body hair, we can 'disrupt some of the silence, invisibility and closure of collusion (even, or especially, if unintended) with capitalist patriarchy,' as Karin Lesnik-Oberstein suggests in her work *The Last Taboo: Women and Body Hair*. And then, with that informed knowledge about the hairy truths (pun intended), feel free to pluck as you please. Or not.

If we look back as far as 1871 to Darwin's *Descent of Man*, it's clear that the world of science was infatuated with racial differences in hair, from its texture and growth to its appearance. This caused the shift in the broader Western psyche about body hair.[1] With body hair being associated with our 'primitive ancestry', what also came with it was the notion that body hair was for the 'less developed', in Darwin's words. What also came with Darwin's evolutionary theory was that the male body was expected to be hairier than the female body and, inevitably, it didn't take long for the capitalist world to latch on to this.

Now don't get me wrong, there was hair removal going on way before this. Apparently as far back as the Stone Age, we had cavemen removing their body hair with sharp objects to prevent frostbite and lice, but I guess you could say this was more for practical reasons than aesthetics. In Ancient Egypt, however, body hair indicated your class status, with body hair being a sign of belonging to an uncivilized and lower class, so not too far off Darwin's theory. Like the Egyptians, the Romans also considered body hair as a class indicator. However, here we find that the notion was more gendered, with the removal adopted by high-class Roman women. But it was in the early twentieth century that this gendered form of social control really took over.

At the dawn of the swinging 1920s, a brand we all know too well, Gillette, created their first razor for women, which promised to save women from their 'embarrassing personal problem'. They took advantage of women now wearing sleeveless tops and shorter skirts and announced that 'Milady Décolleté' is the 'dainty little Gillette used by the well-groomed woman to keep the underarm white and smooth'.[2] Two words that specifically bug me out from that advert. You guessed it. *Dainty* . . . And *white*. I guess it's because our beauty ideals aren't looking too different more than a century later. This construction of what 'femininity' looks like began to ingrain itself in our collective psyches. A woman's body should be dainty, small, seen and not heard. It should be white, smooth and hairless. The brown body is anything but these things, it's an unrealistic beauty standard we are attempting to mould ourselves into, and at the end of the day, that's great for capitalism. We try and keep up with an unrealistic beauty standard that we can never live up to, we keep spending and spending, and the profit-maximizing capitalist system keeps on winning. According to a report by Transparency Market Research, body hair removal is predicted to become a $1.35 billion industry by 2022, with China and India in the lead in the Asian market. So, we tweeze and pluck and wax and press in the hope that we can reach this feminine ideal, but we never will. And more importantly, we shouldn't have to, with emphasis on the word *have*. You can choose to if you wish, but you don't *have* to.

Advertising has changed a lot since the early Gillette advert. New razor brand Billie is putting body hair at the front and centre of their advertising and marketing, with a diverse array of models showing off their body hair, from armpit hair to snail trails. Their online campaign #projectbodyhair attempts to normalize the visibility of body hair, 'because womankind is both shaggy and smooth'. I know this seems a little ironic considering they themselves are trying to sell razors, but I guess at least the messaging is going in the right direction. The new Gillette Venus ads make efforts to convey the same messaging, with a recent one showing black and brown bodies, of different sizes, with stretch marks and scars. Still hairless though. My inner dilemma over the years lies with the fact that the same beauty culture that once made me hate my own body is now telling me that I should embrace it. And that feels kind of strange. I'm being told it's 'my choice', but really, is the 'right choice' still to remove all hair? Is this idea of 'choice' actually an illusion? Perhaps these are the questions we all need to unpack. Under what conditions are we choosing to keep or remove our body hair? Are we *really* making a choice to remove body hair for ourselves, or to satisfy the male gaze? Will we face social punishments if we choose not to conform to what we are told a 'normal' body looks like?

The point is, it's not really a 'choice' if there is only one acceptable option. I believe it will truly be a choice when both hairy and hairless bodies are just simply normalized, especially for bodies of colour. I was recently shocked to see a No7 advert featuring a model with a visible moustache on her upper lip and dark sideburns. The model herself was a woman of colour. I genuinely had to rewind the advert to confirm what I had seen. What I appreciated the most was that it was just an eye-cream advert and nothing to do with her hair. Just eye-cream. I guess this is what normalizing body hair could look like for beauty brands. It made me feel seen. It made me feel normal.

## Hair me roar

Around the same time that my relationship with my body hair loomed large, in my early twenties, I also saw an inspiring Sikh woman named Balpreet Kaur making global headlines. Balpreet is a baptized Sikh who keeps her *kesh* (unshorn hair). Balpreet was waiting in line at the Ohio State University Library when a man took a photo of her without her consent and uploaded it to Reddit, posting it in the 'funny' category because of her visible facial hair. He tagged it with the heading: 'I'm not sure what to conclude from this'. FYI, his username was 'european_douche-bag' – which said a lot. What happened next was inspiring. Balpreet replied to the thread and chose to use it as an opportunity to educate him – and all readers of the thread. She said: 'I'm a baptized Sikh woman with facial hair. Yes, I realize that my gender is often confused and I look different than most women. However, baptized Sikhs believe in the sacredness of this body – it is a gift that has been given to us by the Divine Being (which is genderless, actually) and must keep it intact as a submission to the divine will.' Reading her reply gave me goosebumps. The Reddit user apologized and in his public post said: 'It makes a whole lot of sense to work on having a legacy and not worrying about what you look like. I made that post for stupid internet points and I was ignorant.'

Later, in an article for the *Guardian*, she explained why she chose to use this as an opportunity to spread light, not hate. 'I cannot stop people from forming convoluted first impressions based on what I look like, but I can stop them from turning that ignorance into misplaced assumptions or even hatred [. . .] We Kaurs are strong enough to know that these words do not define us, but our actions and reactions do.' Those last words kept circulating in my mind – other people's opinions won't define me, but my actions and reactions will. If I allow hatred to sit inside me, the only person I'll be harming is myself.

A few years later, I began to see images of body-confidence

advocate, model and influencer, Harnaam Kaur. Harnaam, like myself, was diagnosed with PCOS when she was a teenager, which led her to have more body hair, most noticeably on her face. After years of bullying and abuse, she decided to embrace it and is now widely known as 'the bearded lady'. She is quoted in the *Huffington Post* saying, 'My mum and dad didn't want me to do it – they didn't think I'd be able to have a normal life if I had a beard. They worried I wouldn't be able to get married and that I'd never get a job. But I wanted to make my own decisions and live for myself – not anyone else.' Being featured in the likes of *Glamour*, *Cosmo* and *Teen Vogue* has led to Harnaam speaking to teenagers and adults alike about diversity and self-acceptance.

In a similar way, Instagram pages like 'Brown Girl Gazing' have been using the digital space to talk about women's relationships with their bodies and to 're-define beauty'. The page is filled with gorgeous portraits of brown women, with everything from stretch marks, acne scars, vitiligo to, of course, body hair. These images reminded me that I wasn't alone in my hairy brown journey, and if these women taught me anything, it was that being in this brown body makes me even more powerful.

Despite social media being a great place in which marginalized women like ourselves can feel seen and heard, especially concerning our bodies, it can also be a dangerous place too. As I've been writing this chapter over the last couple of weeks, I've been conducting a lot of online research, including reading articles and journals and watching videos on all things body-hair related. Soon, I noticed that all of my social media feeds started to fill up with ads promoting hair removal products and devices. Thankfully, I was aware that this was due to the dangerous digital algorithms at play. It just goes to show that even a harmless Google search might go on to influence you into looking at and then buying a consumer product you never even wanted in the first place and, potentially, make you feel even worse about your body. What I fear is that younger and more vulnerable women might be more susceptible to this. So, it can only help if inspirational brown women use their social media feeds to show young brown girls that brown bodies are beautiful too. Women like Harnaam, or fashion model Neelam Gill, the first Indian model featured in a Burberry campaign, Simran Randhawa, or Bishamber Das, Britain's first Asian plus-size model, or Mariah Idrissi, H&M's first hijab-wearing model.

In Kim Bansi's awesome mini-documentary called *Ditch the Razor* for UNiDAYs, a student-focused brand and market research consultancy, she highlights the fact that '. . . with social media, you have it in your hand 100 per cent of the time. As you're scrolling through, you see a hundred times more images than we used to see [in magazines].' Kim makes a really valid point here – are millennials and Gen Zs suffering more with the same old, outdated views about body hair because the enforcer is literally in their hands? You only need to look at the documentary's comment section to read 'this is buttas' from one user to see that harmful views about body hair are still alive and kicking. I scrolled down further to find another user felt the need to give their warped understanding of feminism with the words '. . . the thing that separates men from women is that they are more beautiful, clean and can have children. Feminism isn't empowering women it's making women more like men. Wake up gals you're being brainwashed. We are equal in worth and that's all that matters, you guys are just trying to be men instead of women.' You can probably hear my eyes rolling to the back of my head just reading it.

Speaking of men. I know that I am centring much of this conversation around body hair on the brown woman's body, but brown men have skin in the game too (pun definitely intended). The hair on their bodies has been up for contention, particularly in the post 9/11 world, as racially profiled men with beards – specifically Muslim and Sikh men – have been subject to violent abuse. The number of Islamophobic hate crimes jumped seventeen-fold in 2001 and have never returned to levels reported before 9/11.[3] One of the first hate crimes, just four days after, was the murder of Balbir Singh Sodhi, who had a beard and wore a turban as a practising Sikh. The attacker had reportedly told a waiter at a restaurant that 'I'm going to go out and shoot some towel heads.'[4] It just goes to show how the hair on brown bodies can be seen as such a threat to the status quo.

While man buns and beards become all the rage in hipster fashion, brown men haven't been able to participate with the same luxury or ease. Considering the events of recent years, perhaps we could use these examples as a starting point for a dialogue with brown men about our body hair – because it's impacting them too. They too are dealing with the fact that brown bodies have become artefacts of social and political control.

### The three bodies

Medical anthropologists Nancy Scheper-Hughes and Margaret M. Lock would call this kind of regulated and controlled body the 'third body' or the 'body politic'. Now before I lose you, let me try and break down how their article, 'The Mindful Body', written in 1987, and their three perspectives of the body can be applied to body hair. The first body is known as the 'individual body'. This is how you perceive your own body, how you feel about your own body and how your body is personally experienced. It's basically all about you. The second body, otherwise known as the 'social body', is more about how your body builds relationships with nature, society, culture, and maybe even your faith. Finally, as we saw above, there is the third body/body politic, which refers to the 'regulation, surveillance, and control of bodies (individual and collective)'. As Scheper-Hughes and Lock emphasize, 'the body politic can, of course, exert its control over individual bodies in less dramatic and mundane, but no less brutal, ways'[5] – like telling us what we should and shouldn't do with our body hair. In the Western world, everything is very much centred around this third political body, with everything from the size of our bodies to our body hair being regulated, analysed and controlled. The sooner we recognize this, the better. As soon as you become conscious of this fact, you'll start to look at everything a little bit differently. You'll begin to look at adverts a bit differently. Why are we letting oppressive structures like patriarchy and capitalism regulate and control our bodies and tell us how to feel about them? If we could only focus more on the individual and social body, as many Eastern cultures do, we would start to feel better about ourselves, more in tune with our bodies and maybe even our body hair.

During the COVID-19 outbreak in 2020, for the first time in years salons and beauty parlours were shut. A WhatsApp group with some of my girlfriends conveyed an initial sense of panic. 'What am I going to do without my eyebrow lady!?' . . .

'Resorting back to the shower shaves,' said another friend. But over time, this concern seemed to wane. One friend recognized how much money she was saving. 'I've saved about £800!' she told me. For some of these women, it was the first time they were revealing their body hair in their homes, in front of their partners, in front of their families, rather than feeling perpetually dissatisfied with their body in its natural state. Women were saying hello to their hair again and they were OK with it. Priyanka Joshi, a writer and mum to two super girls, told me, 'Fuzzy hair and arms are becoming the new norm. I was speaking to my sister-in-law about this, we remove it mostly for fear of what other people will say, when in reality nobody actually gives a toss. A little longer between removals really doesn't matter. More important things to be concerning ourselves with right now!' If the pandemic showed us anything, it was that there are bigger things to worry about. Hair removal – non-essential. Surviving the pandemic and staying healthy – essential.

As I mentioned at the start of the chapter, I've had laser hair removal done in the past. Despite it being advertised as such, even laser hair removal isn't permanent. You are meant to go for follow-up appointments in subsequent years, but I never really did. I just couldn't see the point anymore. Now I've started to see some of my little friends reappear again, and I greet them with joy. Not shame. When I'm feeling cold, I remind myself that my little hairs play an important role in regulating my body temperature. The muscles surrounding my hair follicles encourage the hairs to stand up – they're giving me a standing ovation to trap more heat near my body, cheering me on, even when I wasn't cheering myself. Sometimes I still feel insecure and remove it. It's a journey. Whether I choose to remove it or not, I continuously remind myself that it is a part of me. The question is whether the choice to remove it is ours, and not a result of the external factors at play. Or because our partners think it's gross. Or because capitalism and body politics want us to spend our money to make us feel better.

## Different shades, different treatment

This slow but powerful journey of coming to believe that our brown bodies are normal and beautiful requires us to challenge uncomfortable truths in all their forms. Because sometimes we go further than trying to remove our thick dark hair. Sometimes we even want to alter the brown skin it sits upon. From being told not to spend too much time in the sun to using skin-lightening creams, to experiencing outright discrimination, skin colour bias within the brown community has a long-standing history of toxicity. And it's called colourism.

Colourism (or spelt colorism by our friends over the Atlantic) was first coined by American novelist and activist Alice Walker, in her 1980s essay collection *In Search of Our Mothers' Gardens: Womanist Prose*. In the essay 'If the Present Looks Like the Past, What Does the Future Look Like?' she describes colourism as 'The prejudicial or preferential treatment of same-race people based solely on their color.' Whereas racism, which we are all familiar with, usually comes from another ethnic group, colourism can come from both outside and within our own communities. Many people would like to believe that these skin tone biases were established and encouraged during British colonial rule but, unfortunately, it predates even that. Sonali Johnson, from the Department of Gender and Women's Health at the World Health Organization, suggested that it began as far back as the conquest of dark-skinned Dravidians by fair-skinned Aryan migrants from Central Asia/Eastern Europe, probably around 1500 BCE.[6] She proposes: 'It is generally understood that the caste system was introduced by this nomadic group, and was based on the concept of varna or colour, where the light-skinned Aryans used this racial structure to separate themselves from the conquered dark, indigenous population.' However, some historians suggest that this 'Aryan Invasion Theory', as it's been coined, was a theory cooked up by Europeans to justify their own rule centuries later.

Whether that is true or not, two things we know are certain. Number one, you can't have a conversation about colourism without casteism. And number two is that when the Portuguese, Dutch and British made their way east, a caste and class hierarchy structure, with skin colour woven in, definitely existed. And they took advantage of it. They would champion people with lighter skin, whilst portraying those with darker skin as uncivilized untouchables, pitting groups against one another. Dalit women are still suffering from the effects of caste-based violence to this day, facing higher risks of gender-based violence, sexual violence and economic deprivation. It's a perfect example of divide and conquer, and this continued right up until independence and partition in 1947. What came with this was the dominance of Eurocentric beauty standards, with the fair white woman becoming the ideal.[7] And this unfair standard became so deeply ingrained that it still exists today.

Cosmetic companies jumped at the chance to create products that would assist brown women's anxious desire to reach this self-destructive ideal. According to Zion Market Research, the global skin-lightening products market is expected to reach $8.9 billion by 2024. Imagine young brown girls seeing these products in their mother's bathroom cabinet or on TV screens. What is it telling them about their own skin? What impact could it have on their self-esteem? What is it telling them about those with darker skin than theirs? Could it even plant a seed of colourism and racism?

One of the leading names in the game was Unilever's Fair & Lovely which launched back in 1978, a range including everything from soap to face creams under the banner. Unilever is ranked as the fourth-largest consumer goods company in the world. If you have a look at the back of some of the cosmetics products lying around your house, you're bound to find their name. As of June 2020, Unilever renamed its product after two online petitions created a backlash against it for promoting negative stereotypes around dark skin tones. Now don't get it twisted, the product still exists, just under a new name – Glow & Lovely. Ugh, I know. Johnson & Johnson made a better move, altogether halting the sale of the Clean & Clear Fairness line, which had been widely available in Asia and the Middle East. And if you're thinking this is a faraway problem, think again. These products are being sold over the counter and under the counter at Asian stores here in the UK and are still easily available online. Now I know these cosmetics companies did not create colourism, but they are part of the reason it continues. If we stop fuelling the fire with our consumer dollar, we can reduce the demand for these products, and they wouldn't be made in the first place. As long as the demand is there, they'll just keep going. A little rebranding here, a little change in marketing there, but with the underlying message that 'lighter skin is better' still there.

It is these types of systemic ideals that have also led to an inherent, toxic level of anti-blackness within Asian communities. After years of serving under the oppressive nature of British rule, we became conditioned to believe that our lighter-than-black-people skin made us superior to those darker than us. These views have become entrenched. Just like Kamal Al-Solaylee noted in his work *Brown*, 'brown people can turn their in-between skin into a back door to Europeans and whiteness.' And he's right. But what I'd like to further emphasize is that the brownness-over-blackness superiority complex will only ever get you through the 'back door', as Kamal said. Don't even think about trying to get through the front door. You will never be seen as white, or equal to them, so don't get it twisted. As much as you might assimilate into white society, or denounce communities darker than you, they will always see you as the 'Other' too. We've all been fooled into believing that we will climb our way up the lighter skin hierarchy, rather than rejecting it altogether. So quit the colourism and the anti-blackness, ASAP, and call it out if you, unfortunately, have to witness it.

After the death of George Floyd in May 2020, the Black Lives Matter campaign helped us confront anti-blackness in our own living rooms, forcing both young and old to deconstruct their biases about the black community. At the time, I saw some members of the brown community cry out online, 'What about us though? We have to deal with racism too . . .' or adopting the 'all lives matter' approach. As understandable as this sentiment might seem, when a specific community needs our support, we need to give it to them, and not make it about us. I find the 'burning house' analogy really helpful here. When a house is burning, you wouldn't say, 'Well, what about my house?' You would go and help the house in need. (Hopefully!) Yes, we have all been victims of white supremacism. But that should be even more of a reason to look out for marginalized or oppressed communities when they need us to show up, rather than further isolating them by making it about us, or perpetuating the problem by being anti-black ourselves.

## Agents of change

So how can we show up, I hear you say? As well as having these conversations within our homes, we could use our voice and platform in other ways, just like Sharan Dhaliwal, the founder of the *Burnt Roti* magazine. Sharan dedicated the third issue of the magazine to the theme of anti-blackness in South Asian communities, featuring essays, artwork and photography. Another example is the online campaign #BollywoodSoWhite, launched after the highly problematic Bollywood song 'Beyoncé Sharma Jayegi' came out – a song that featured popular Bollywood actors Ananya Panday and Ishaan Khatter, and included the lyrics 'Oh tujhe dekh ke goriya, Beyoncé sharma jayegi'. This roughly translates as 'Beyoncé will feel insecure after seeing you, fair-skinned lady' (the song was stupidly misogynistic too). Popular social media influencer Sheerah called out the stupidity on her Instagram page. 'Bollywood has consistently endorsed self-hatred and anti-Blackness, perpetuating violent white/Indo Aryan supremacist ideologies that harm Black and Dark-skinned South Asian Folx through movies, music etc.' She went on to say to her followers, 'I encourage anyone and everyone to use the #BollywoodSoWhite hashtag. Pen your letters, thoughts to Bollywood to hold them accountable, apologize and start to make change.' This is how we can show up. Sheerah, who describes herself as a 'hairy darksknd tamil Dravidian immigrant' on Instagram, has been using her online platform to challenge anti-blackness and colourism. Her feed is filled with her own gorgeous images, unapologetically conveying the beauty of her dark skin and body hair. She was also featured in Beyoncé's 'Brown Skinned Girl' music video.

Another brown girl showing up is Nina Davuluri. Back in 2014, Nina Davuluri became the first Miss America to be of Indian descent. Sadly, what came with her win were not only racist remarks like being called 'Miss Al Qaeda' or 'Miss Terrorist' but several comments about her skin tone. The next day, she woke up to find front-page headlines reading 'Is Miss America too Dark to be Miss India?' implying that she would never have won such a prize if she had lived on the Asian continent. Since her win, Nina has been using her platform to campaign against the manufacture of skin-whitening products and their harmful advertising, as well as carrying out advocacy work in STEM education. She is currently working on a docu-series entitled *COMPLEXion*, where she has been interviewing people from around the world on their experiences of colourism.

Brown women are trying to shift the status quo in all kinds of industries. See make-up artist and content creator Karishma Leckraz, for example, who has also been playing her part in the beauty community. She told Radio 1 *Newsbeat* that she started using skin-whitening products aged thirteen – 'I was told that I have "such pretty features", but it's a shame I'm "so dark". She said, 'If I could go back, I'd tell my younger self to stop straight away and not even think about using creams like that.' Karishma, who also suffers from atopic eczema, has been doing an incredible job at using her role within the beauty industry to challenge toxic beauty standards.

It is these kinds of actions, whether big or small, online, in our work or in the home, that will continue to make a difference to our generation and those who come after us. Hetal Lakhani, an old friend of mine who now lives in Dallas, called out the matrimonial site Shaadi.com for launching a 'skin-colour' filter. The uproar started when user Meghan Nagpal was searching the website to find a potential life partner and came across a filter which included 'Fair', 'Whitish' and 'Dark' as options. When Meghan reached out to the matrimonial site, one representative replied that 'most parents do require this as an option, so it's visible on the site.' Hetal was shocked, and so launched a petition via Change.org which received hundreds of signatures in a matter of hours.

Maybe the website was right about one thing, and that was that skin colour bias does exist when parents are attempting to find potential suitors for their children. Itisha Nagar found in her research, *The Unfair Selection: A Study on Skin Color Bias in Arranged Indian Marriages*, that there is still an 'overriding importance of skin-color' when it comes to matchmaking. In her study, she showed mothers photographs of a 'highly attractive fair girl/boy or a highly attractive dark girl/boy' as potential partners for their own child. The images were in fact of the same person but just edited. When the mothers were asked which ones they would recommend as partners for their own children, you guessed it, they all picked the fair-skinned photographs! Itisha's study proved her hypothesis that the 'Photograph of dark-skinned individual will receive lower ratings than equally attractive and qualified fair-skinned individual.' A day after Hetal's petition, Shaadi.com posted on Twitter that the filter was a 'blind spot' and that it had been removed. Win!

These online discussions about colourism really had me doing some self-reflection. I began thinking about how young I was when I first experienced the glorification of pale skin. I was probably around the age of six or seven when I first heard aunties saying that we girls shouldn't spend too much time playing in the sun. But to be honest, it's probably even earlier than that. As soon as a baby pops out, whether it is said out loud or saved for auntie gossip for another time, people love to comment on the fairness or otherwise of a brown baby. From that moment onwards, we keep pushing white standards of beauty and femininity onto them. Maybe that's why I kept writing short stories about Hannah and Sarah, with their blonde hair, blue eyes and, obviously, white skin. Maybe when brown girls heard the evil queen in *Snow White* say, 'Mirror, mirror on the wall, who's the fairest of them all?' it was an all too familiar cry. And it's here that I want to flag up a really important point. I recognize, as I'm of North Indian descent, I am a lighter-skinned brown girl. I acknowledge that puts me in a position of privilege; some things will come easier for me than for my darker sisters. And it is with that consciousness I wish to do better and to never perpetuate, ignore, or deny the struggle of darker sisters because there will be no collective progression for the brown sisterhood if anyone is left behind.

## Saying bye to beauty standards

Even when skin-whitening products get left in the past, there might be another obstacle to tackle or another crappy ideal to fight, so it's more important than ever that the brown sisterhood has each other's backs. Sooner rather than later, we'll have to have conversations about how the digital age and the likes of filters on social media are also contributors to our facial dysmorphia. Obviously, these are issues experienced not just by brown women, but women of all races, and, increasingly, many men. I'm talking about the 'beauty' filters that lighten or darken your skin, depending on what's in fashion, smooth out your pores, gloss and plump your lips and zap away your eye bags. What once consisted of funny animal masks, dogs drooping their tongues out or a bedazzled crown on your head have now morphed into unrealistic face filters. In Chapter 9, I'll be discussing why reducing our screen time might be a way to tackle these never-ending obstacles. The point is, every time we remove one toxic product targeting women's bodies, and especially brown bodies, another one pops up, just like in that whack-a-mole game that you used to play at arcades.

Do you want to know the irony in all this colourism malarky? As the rich get richer, they want to get darker and more tanned. As we get richer, we cry to be whiter. In the West, skin-tanning has now come to signify the privilege of having leisure time and luxury in the sun's rays on the beach or, alternatively, the money to pay for a sunbed visit. It just goes to show that beauty trends are forever changing, and there will always be people trying to capitalize on it. Be it skin tones, be it hair or no hair, be it thin eyebrows or thick eyebrows, be it curvy or thin, beauty standards get invented, altered, recycled and changed again. There are more contortions in the beauty myth standards than in a jalebi. It's so confusing. Anything to do with aesthetics can change over time or according to the cultural context, so if the trends are forever changing, what can we brown women do? Do we keep changing and morphing our bodies every time the trend changes? Because I don't want to feel like a jalebi.

Isn't it about time that I tell little Jaspreet, getting ready for her friend's birthday party, to disrupt the lessons that taught her that pain is beauty and beauty is pain, and to redefine her own beauty? And that the brown body, in all its forms, shapes, colours and sizes, is also a normal body. So far, I hope this book has started to help us all figure out how to give ourselves – and all women – a strong sense of identity that has nothing to do with our physical appearance. Remember, it's never too late to learn and unlearn. Your identity is full of treasures. Maybe some of that treasure is sitting in the roots of our hair or in the melanin in our skin? I can only hope that there will come a day when brown girls, including myself, will feel fully confident in their unaltered brown body. But until then, whether you decide to remove your body hair or keep it, whether you choose to lighten your skin or not, just make sure whatever choice you make with the outside of your body is true to you. Not for no guy, not for no auntie and not for no dumb beauty standard. Remember, your body was your first friend, on the inside and out. So, don't hate her.

# CHAPTER 6

# SARI, NOT SORRY

*The Cultural Appropriation Conversation*

*maybe i'm wrong to assume*
*that the same mouths that made the word*
*immigrant*
*so dirty*
*are the same mouths craving for a curry on a friday night*
*– or a chai tea latte?*

Mum and I were having our usual five o'clock cup of tea: Tesco Value Nice biscuits on the table, my nephews running around the living room, the TV on in the background. Our daily cha* catch-ups had become something of a routine during my early twenties, but it hadn't always been that way. As an adolescent, my relationship with my mum was tricky. I was a book-smart but rebellious teenager, keen to explore the ways of other people my age and, in some sense, denying my culture, who I was and where I came from. On the other hand, my mum wanted to keep me close to my roots, reminding me of who I was and where I came from, which I often rejected. It was only as I got older that I started to take some pride in parts of my culture. We'll come back to that a little bit later.

At some point during our daily catch-up, Iggy Azalea's music video 'Bounce' appeared on the screen. She was wearing a red *lengha* with gold embroidery, a *tikka* resting on her forehead, a *dupatta* draped across her head and a group of Bollywood back-up dancers behind her. In case you aren't aware, Azalea is not a Bollywood actress. She is a white Australian rapper. My

* Some brown folk say cha, some say chai. Nearly all of the words for tea in the world fall into three broad groups: *te*, *cha* and *chai*, which all derived from China. The Chinese character for tea is 茶. If you're a tea lover like me, you can find out more in Victor H. Mair and Erling Hoh, *The True History of Tea* (Thames & Hudson, 2009) pp. 262–4

mum glanced at the screen and said, 'Doesn't she look nice in that lengha.' I didn't really think much of her comment at the time, Mum has always been a fan of seeing what new styles were in – whether velvet had come back in fashion, what new colours were on-trend. It was only when she made her next comment that I started to pay more attention. 'I wish I could have worn them more when I was her age . . .'

It broke my heart. I began to see the double standards that existed around fashion, how a culture that I once thought was too foreign for Western eyes had suddenly become trendy, a culture I had grown up denying. In that moment, I felt so sad. In that moment, I understood the meaning of cultural appropriation. And more importantly, I understood what it felt like.

My mum migrated to the UK in 1977 at the age of eighteen, to marry my dad. Mum had been travelling to college on a local school bus in Jalandhar, Punjab, when Dad's auntie first saw her. I'm not surprised that Dad's auntie became besotted by Mum on that bus and thought she'd be the perfect match for my dad who was already settled in the UK at the time. Mum was, and still is, absolutely stunning. A long brown plait was hidden under her dupatta, big brown eyes, a long, pointy Punjabi nose, and a book bag which indicated to the auntie that she was smart and came from a good home. It wasn't long after that that my dad's family came to meet my mum's mum, who we'll hear more about in the next chapter. She had been a widow for almost fifteen years at the time, and was obviously over the moon to hear of the marriage proposal. If her daughter moved to England, she could have the chance of a better life. The marriage and wedding preparations began, and Mum flew over to the UK in August 1977, her first time on an aeroplane. She had only ever seen my dad's photograph. Dad must have been a right looker, or maybe it was his seventies fashion sense that had Mum swooning! Anyhow, Dad picked her up from the airport (after first approaching the wrong woman), and they got married in October that same year. They have looked after each other ever since.

Like most first-wave immigrant families, they found those early years very tough. Mum spent her days working the till in our corner shop in east London (I know, I know – ticking off that brown corner shop stereotype already), whilst Dad worked two other jobs. Acceptance of differences was still in its early days during the 1970s in east London, so Mum had to constantly try to ignore the murmurs of 'Paki' under so many breaths and the sniggers about how she dressed. Soon her salwar kameez had to stay home; instead, she saved up enough spare change to buy herself a pair of jeans on sale in Marks & Spencer and wore my dad's Naf Naf jacket every single day. It became her new armour. It was clear that to assimilate into the British culture, there was no space for her salwar kameez. It was too different, too colourful, too brash. Too foreign.

## Givers and takers

Now, let's fast forward into the present day . . . When someone shows up to a Halloween party with blackface or brownface, wears a turban on a runway as an accessory, or wears a lengha in a music video with Bollywood back-up dancers, these offensive cultural stereotypes are minimizing the struggles and real-life issues that many people face daily. These microaggressions are often accompanied by comments meant to disarm the anger, such as 'it's fashion' or 'it's just a joke', which often reveal the lack of empathy and the insensitivity that non-people-of-colour have towards these issues. As brown folk, we have a right to be upset and offended when someone dresses like a 'Bollywood beauty', when we were never allowed to because it made us 'too different'.

South Asian culture has also been a source of, shall we say, 'style inspiration' for celebrities such as Katy Perry, Kim Kardashian, Ivanka Trump ... the list goes on. Recently, a well-known online fashion brand was slammed for selling hair accessories that they called the 'chandelier head clip'. The accessory is, in fact, a tikka that I could buy for a quarter of the price on Southall Broadway. To add further insult to injury, the site decided that bindis were a Halloween accessory. The uproar from consumers forced the company to remove the selection of bindis. But can you blame these stores and brands wanting to sell them? When I was a teenager during the nineties, bands like No Doubt made bindis the new cool accessory, thanks to Gwen Stefani. There is no doubt (no pun intended) that celebrities have a role to play within the messy appropriation world.

So why does it hurt? Is it because people wearing costumes such as these take our culture and condense it into a single-faceted – and often stereotypical – image that is both derivative and ignorant? With the ever-growing need for likes and retweets on social media, will this racial fetishization of the exotic continue to grow? I can understand that there might be confusion over what's OK and not OK. Is this going to get worse before it gets better? And if so, how can we educate and challenge those around us? How can we make sure that we, brown women, are leading the conversation in how we want our cultures to be portrayed?

Some people suggest that cultural appropriation isn't as critical as other issues within racial and cultural oppression. Direct violence, abuse and brutality are more urgent. Discussion around cultural appropriation can sometimes even seem like another way to make barriers when we should be making bridges. But, as we look more closely, not only will the cultural appropriation conversation build more understanding and empathy for other cultures, but we'll see how it acts as another clear example of the deep-rooted inequality in the history of cultural exchange. If we keep dismissing the impact of cultural appropriation, are we prioritizing the feelings and desires of people of power and privilege over the rights of minorities?

Cities within the Western world have often operated on the paradoxical basis that while diversity is what makes a city like my hometown, London, great, the minorities within such cities are barred from many of the positions and rights that white citizens have historically been able to enjoy. Cultural appropriation is an example of this unjust dynamic, and it is a method by which minorities are seen as inferior because their cultures are defined as 'foreign' by others. Cultural appropriation is rooted in white privilege and systemic oppression. Those in positions of power can cherry pick which elements of a minority culture they like and don't like. In doing so, the meaning and importance behind these cultural elements are often lost and reduced to a simple fashion statement, as we've seen above.

Cultural appropriation is a bit like a brown girl doing a test and getting a C+, then a white girl copying her answers and getting an A. I'll never forget the time when I was in Year 5, and I returned to school after my sister's wedding in the Easter holidays with henna patterns still flowing on my hands. The white girl sitting next to me in class said: 'Ugh, don't come near me, I don't want to catch your rash! You're diseased!' Later that year, the same girl came back from a family trip to Goa, with her hands covered in henna patterns, and all the other girls went apeshit at how pretty it was. When I spoke to Rimla Akhtar MBE, chair of the Muslim Women's Sports Foundation, about some of these examples of cultural appropriation, she described the situation as 'frustratingly ironic . . .' She said: 'When we do it [our cultural items], we're seen as "lesser". Backwards. When they [white people] do it, it's suddenly a new fashion trend, mysterious and exotic . . .'

Cultural appropriation is a term that was added to the *Oxford English Dictionary* in early 2017. It refers to the 'adoption of certain elements of a society by members of another, *usually dominant* society.' By definition, cultural appropriation is actually a noun. But I feel it's a verb. It is something that is done to us, an action performed consciously or unconsciously. Obviously, cultural appropriation is nothing new. Specifically, for the South Asian community, forms of appropriation began as early as the seventeenth century when Europeans first began colonizing parts of Asia. Things that were once considered savage and uncivilized, like our food, customs, bright colours and clothes, suddenly became all the rage. Enjoyed, commodified, sold and profited from – all whilst we stood with empty pockets, empty stomachs and a growing self-hatred. And though the days of the British Empire are long gone, the internalized self-hate and pain that colonized people developed will take a while to unlearn.

References to cultural appropriation were found back in 1979, in sociologist Dick Hebdige's book *Subculture: The Meaning of Style.* He looked at how white subcultures in Great Britain constructed 'style' to reinforce communal identity and borrowed cultural or revolutionary symbols from other marginalized groups. For example, punk style borrows heavily from Rastafarian culture and working-class apparel. The key to understanding what cultural appropriation is is to understand what power structures are at play. Who is cultural appropriation hurting, and why? In the past, the cultural appropriation conversation has been conducted almost entirely by lawyers, anthropologists, museum curators, archaeologists and artists. But the issues haven't really been analysed from a social context, especially for the South Asian diaspora.

For us to fully comprehend how cultural appropriation plays out, I think it's worth understanding different types. In 2008, James Young, a leading contemporary philosopher of art, outlined the forms of cultural appropriation that take place in the arts community, but these apply clearly to South Asian women as well. Firstly, there is *object appropriation*; this would be a possession or a tangible object that has been stolen or, to put it politely, transferred, from one culture to the member of another culture. This could be how we describe Azalea's actions. Young also highlights something called *subject appropriation*, sometimes called voice appropriation. This is when an outsider experiences a culture as if they were insiders. A good example of this is Rudyard Kipling's *Kim* – 'The book presents a vivid picture of India, its teeming populations, religions, and superstitions, and the life of the bazaars and the road.'[1] Kipling was born in India in 1865 and worked as a journalist while writing many of his early works. Still, his perspective as a white man living in India is inevitably very different from those of people of colour. When praising *The Jungle Book*, let us not forget that he is also the man who wrote *The White Man's Burden* and supported General Dyer's actions during the Amritsar Massacre of 1919. Kipling himself was an imperialist. In the context of the time, I suppose it was acceptable for a white man to own the voice of the 'coloured man' and speak about India in this way through his literature. But is it still acceptable today?

## Missing voices

Back then, brown people were seen as illiterate and too inept to tell their own stories, except for a few famous exceptions that proved the rule. Is it still OK for this type of voice appropriation to take place now? For decades, white writers have penned stories about other cultures – this alone isn't a problem, but it becomes a problem when non-white writers telling the same stories with their own voices are denied access to publishing, in favour of those white writers.

Brown writers should be able to write about our own experiences, allowing us to centre our voices in our cultural narrative. But as we've seen, many industries are behind the curve in terms of representation; the publishing and journalism industries being some of the worst offenders.

It's true that the industry has been announcing strategies for change since 2015. Publishing houses have rolled out paid internships, mentoring schemes and traineeships to attract socially under-represented applicants, as well as creating opportunities for women to move into boardrooms. But I guess I'm sometimes torn between optimism about this and the fear that publishing the right skin colour is just a trend, a box to tick, tokenism rather than something that's for the societal good.

What I have found empowering is writers of colour taking things into their own hands so that people don't tell our stories for us. We tell them. The author and writer Nikesh Shukla put together an anthology of writing, *The Good Immigrant*, because he felt these voices were not being heard, and crowdfunded it with the publisher Unbound in 2016. It has showcased a host of new talent and sold 60,000 copies. Nikesh and some of the other writers in the collection have become household names amongst millennial and Gen Z brown readers worldwide! Other examples include #Merky Books, an imprint within William Heinemann over at Penguin, curated by rapper and songwriter Stormzy, and even smaller publishing houses like Kashi House, focusing on publishing books specifically on Sikh and Punjabi heritage.

The brown female voice isn't missing only in writing. The same lack can be seen in theatre, television and film, with Asian women at risk of becoming an invisible minority. Where are they? Where are their roles? Where are their stories? If we aren't telling the stories about our cultures in the way we want to, then who will? The ones that do get to be shown often do really well, so why aren't there more? Standouts like Gurinder Chadha's *Bend It Like Beckham* and Mindy Kaling's *The Mindy Project* resonated widely with brown women worldwide, but they can't be the only ones? These voices are missing both in front of the camera and behind it. There are hardly any brown women producers, directors, screenwriters and story commissioners. According to Dr Stacy L. Smith from the USC Annenberg Inclusion Initiative, out of the top 1,300 movies in the last thirteen years, only 11 of them were directed by a woman of colour. Everywhere you look these days, whether it's the Oscars or the

Golden Globes, people are crying out for more meaningful representation and recognition, and diverse storytelling.

If we were telling our own stories, if we decided how we wanted our cultures to be portrayed, then would that make us the dominant voice?

## Altered images and the white gaze

One of the saddest aspects of this appropriation of brown culture is that even the source community finds fashion more aesthetically appealing on a white body. Back when I was at university, I was scouted for an Asian modelling agency who were looking for models for two big bridal magazine clients. As quite an insecure 5ft 10, gangly, four-eyed, braces-wearing teenager, being approached to be a model at the age of eighteen was super flattering and a major confidence boost. But, sadly, it ended up doing the complete opposite. Photoshoots would usually start early, with make-up and hair starting around 5 a.m. By 7 a.m. the shoot would start, in the hope of getting as much daylight as possible. Three to four outfit and location changes, make-up and hair done again, usually in ridiculous 5-inch heels. No food or water were offered the whole day. It wasn't as glamorous as I thought it would be, and it impacted my self-esteem. I was already underweight at this time, but they still told me I was 'a bit on the larger side' and my hips would require editing. I even remember hearing a man on set telling one of the female stylists to stuff my bra with tissues because my chest was too flat! But this wasn't the worst of it. A few weeks later, I heard the magazine had been released. I rushed to Ilford Lane to one of the shops that was selling it. I desperately sifted through the pages. And there I was. Unrecognizable.

They had thinned me down, but worst of all, *they had lightened my skin*. I looked like a white girl. Not Asian, not brown. White. I then flicked through the rest of the Asian bridal magazine and realized that most other models were white European, often eastern European. To top it all off, I didn't even get paid! So, when a young brown-bride-to-be goes and buys these magazines, they're getting two messages: 1. Brown girls are not beautiful enough or fair enough to be on the cover of magazines; 2. You might be the magazine's target consumer, but they are still going to use white people to sell you the products.

It's so confusing. Imagine that you already had confidence issues from growing up as a young brown girl. Couple this with being so insecure and embarrassed by your culture that you denied it growing up. Imagine only ever seeing models who conformed to Eurocentric beauty standards on the magazine covers, adverts on TV and runways. Imagine, then, seeing all the cultural products you were once denied, or ridiculed for wearing, being flaunted by white women. How confusing!

It's been suggested that one cause of the increased visibility of appropriation has been the digital revolution and subsequent advances in technology, which have produced a tremendous outpouring of creative artistry and commerce. The new technologies encourage anyone and everyone to engage in cutting and pasting, sampling and downloading, and otherwise copying pre-existing works, styles or fashions. Graphic artists like Maria Qamar and Saher (known as the online Pakistani Martha Stewart) have seen their designs copied and used on apparel that appears on websites like Etsy.com without their permission or any recognition. So, on the one hand, while the internet has been great for enabling ethnic minority women to have a voice and take back their narrative, something we'll hear more of in Chapter 9, it has also made cultural appropriation easier and quicker than ever, with fewer or no consequences.

## Unequal cultural exchange

When I've called out cultural appropriation online over the last few years, or when the issue is brought to my attention, I often run into the same arguments, which are basically another form of microaggression: 'But you wear Western clothes, so doesn't that mean YOU'RE appropriating.' Before I smack my head on my keyboard for the tenth time, I usually reply: 'Cultural appropriation is when cultural aspects are adopted by a more dominant society. I, as a young woman of colour, do not fit into the "dominant category" so I don't think I'm stealing anyone's Western clothes.' Minorities have had a long history of having to adopt white language, clothing and behaviour to survive – literally! Sometimes survival means losing a part of your own cultural identity in the process. This is not cultural appropriation; this is what psychiatrist and political philosopher Frantz Fanon would call the process of assimilation. Indeed, even writers such as Rabindranath Tagore and Dwijendra Lal Roy drew freely on ideas from English playwrights. Writing in Hindi, Jaishankar Prasad produced history plays modelled on Shakespeare's work. But we cannot forget that the brown folk were not the superior class here. If anything, they had Western culture thrust upon them. Colonizers and missionaries felt they were 'morally bound' to change the ways of people of colour. The whitewashing of education, faith and the home that happened over decades made it inevitable that Western ideals would make their way into South

Asian art and fashion. These ideals followed the South Asian migrants to the lands that they settled in and meant they tried their hardest to assimilate – for example, my mum buying jeans from Marks & Spencer. We began losing our own culture whilst we assimilated into a new one. So, let's put that one to rest; there is genuinely no such thing as reverse cultural appropriation. White Western people are never discriminated against or teased for wearing Western clothes because it is simply the dominant mainstream culture and normal accepted behaviour. That culture is what we centre on today, what we – unfortunately – peg as the standard against which we measure others.

In May 2019, there was uproar when a brand as big as Gucci started using the turban, hijab and the niqab in one of their campaigns. To put this in context, since the 1950s, Western governments have sought to encourage as much assimilation as possible, encouraging immigrants to abandon their supposedly inferior cultures – a horrifying and short-sighted prospect. What is even more terrifying is seeing brown folk who were brainwashed into agreeing. Sikh Conservative councillor, Mr Mangat, expressed it quite clearly in 1973: 'The best hope for Sikhs in this country lies in abandoning the turban and making themselves as inconspicuous as possible. It would damage community relations and hinder the process of acceptance and integration if Sikhs looked conspicuous in the street.' Can you imagine how Sikh men, and women for that matter, might have felt hearing these kinds of speeches? The fear and anxiety my grandad must have felt walking down the street in Dagenham in his turban when he worked at the Ford Motor Company, even questioning whether he should remove it. Those pains and traumas still live within us. They pass on from generation to generation. It took until 1989 for the UK Employment Act to finally give Sikhs the right to wear a turban in the workplace.

That's why one of the Gucci items, named the 'Indy Full Turban', caused outrage online when it appeared on the American retailer Nordstrom's website, retailing at £790. The Sikh Coalition tweeted that the turban was 'not just a fashion accessory, but also a sacred religious article of faith'. My husband, also coincidentally called Indy, can tell you that you can buy turban material for a fraction of that price at any cloth house in the UK. The item, first previewed in early 2018, is from the same collection as the £689 black 'balaclava' polo neck with red lips that the brand withdrew after complaints of blackface. Alessandro Michele, the creative director, later apologized, saying that: 'From my grief, I will learn something. We will learn a lesson and this company will do things in a different way.' Gucci's chief executive added that the mistake was caused 'because of cultural ignorance, but ignorance is not an excuse.' They eventually hired a new diversity chief.

We've seen similar examples of this with hijabs being worn on the runway as accessory items. Speaking to *HuffPost UK*, Lamisa Khan, a reporter at *Amaliah*, was equally appalled by the use of the hijab and said it was a 'mockery'. Twitter users shared her anger, with one user tweeting, 'My mum gets harassed for wearing the headscarf – and you make your models wear it for fashion. Couldn't you find any actual Muslim/brown people to wear the hijab?'

The painful truth is that despite the commodification of the turban and hijab by big brands, as we saw in Chapter 5, since 9/11, hate crimes towards turban-wearing Sikhs and hijab/niqab-wearing Muslims have, in fact, risen. The horrific mass shooting at Wisconsin Sikh Temple in 2012 or the 375 per cent increase in Islamophobic incidents in 2018, after UK Prime Minister Boris Johnson compared Muslim women to 'letterboxes',[2] are the reality for turban- or headscarf-wearing people. Even ten-year-old Sikh girl Munsimar Kaur was told, 'No, you can't play, because you're a terrorist,' by a group of teenagers in a park in Plumstead, London, in the summer of 2019.[3] Despite this horrible remark, the next day, Munsimar plucked up the courage to return to the park and made a new friend. About an hour later, her new friend's mum called her away and told her not to play with Munsimar because she was 'dangerous'.

Are we really 'equally exchanging' our cultures if a brown woman is scared to go out of the house in salwar kameez, hijab, burqa or turban because of our current political climate, but a white woman can safely go to a music festival in similar cultural or religious items and not feel a slight sense of fear?

During my interview with Milly, a sixth-form student from London, she described her experience of this kind of unequal exchange: 'I work at a coffee shop, and I wear the hijab full-time, even at work! It was a cold morning, and a white lady came into the shop and said, "I wish I wore what you're wearing on your head, it must be keeping you warm." I smiled and said, "It is, but so is God's happiness with me for wearing it." She looked confused. I felt uncomfortable in this situation because the true meaning of why I wear the hijab was stripped away. It's not to keep my ears warm but rather to remember God in everything that I do, and respect my religion always . . .' In isolation, this situation may seem harmless, but in combination with several other microaggressions, comments and looks that Milly has to face on a daily basis, you can understand why this unequal exchange can be frustrating. All those paper cuts . . .

When I spoke to Sheeza Shah, founder and CEO of UpEffect, a crowdfunding and support platform for companies improving the planet and human lives, she suggested that much of this unequal exchange is down to our current political climate. Sheeza also said: 'As a UK resident, seeing my neighbours elect a Prime Minister who compares niqab-wearing women with letterboxes is a disturbing reality that I and many other Muslims now live with. This political climate has perpetuated racism and discrimination across all industries, particularly the fashion industry, which profits not only from the exploitation of poor Muslim garment workers, but actively puts hijabs and turbans on their runways while attaching a hefty price tag. The very same people that ridicule the garments that we adopt as Muslims, are capitalizing from our oppression . . .' Sheeza then went on to say that: '. . . it shouldn't come as a surprise to us, after all, capitalism by nature thrives at the expense of society's most vulnerable.'

Not only have the hijab and burqa been appropriated on runways but suddenly overtly sexual depictions of the veil are popping up everywhere. And there's an equally ghastly name for this trend – 'the burqa swag'. From 'Sexy Middle Eastern Arab girl burqa Halloween costume' on eBay to celebrities like Lady Gaga, who have been seen in burqa-like garments for years. For instance, in 2012 she wore a fur niqab to a fashion show. Later at the same event, she walked on a runway in a see-through hot pink burqa, transparent enough to show her bedazzled underwear. Though it's not the usual narrative, it's still blatantly offensive and appropriative, and a clear example of the unequal cultural exchange. Keep in mind that in some parts of the world, wearing a hijab and burqa as a brown woman can get you attacked, or worse, killed.

When it comes to the discussion of protecting aspects of one's culture, I've been at many dinner table conversations that go something like this: 'So, are there legal measures to protect minorities from appropriation?' At the other end of the table, someone interrupts: 'Wait a second – it's the mix of cultures that makes Britain great! Can't we all just borrow from each other's cultures?' Someone else interjects: 'You do know there's no such thing as curry?' to lighten the mood. But as one of the leading scholars in the cultural appropriation space, Susan Scafidi emphasizes in her work *Who Owns Culture* that culture is fluid and evolving. In any case, it would be challenging to establish restrictive forms of ownership or to police cultural borrowing. It just goes to show that the concept of culture is a difficult one to define and has been under attack for many years. Some propose that the concept of culture itself is elitist and imperialist. Some feminists argue that women's achievements and contributions are often ignored when looking at what comprises a group's culture. Despite all these debates, we can't ignore the fact that culture is political, whether we want it to be or not. There are endless debates between the left and the right on multiculturalism, nationalism, Britishness and 'British Values'. How are brown women meant to navigate this, and retain a sense a belonging, whilst also trying to make sure their culture isn't attacked or disrespected?

As consumers, we often define our life experiences and associations through the things we buy (and then by what we upload onto our Instagram feed!). When we go to another country and experience another culture, we often buy a souvenir. When we graduate, we buy a graduation picture (or like my mum, you buy a hundred and give them to all of your relatives). When we go to a concert, we buy a T-shirt. What is interesting is that, when these cultural products are readily available to us, we lose interest in understanding where they actually come from. The fact that Asian culture has become so commodified and so easy to access means that people are less invested in understanding what it is or where it comes from.

So, what can we do? What can we do better, as individuals, as consumers, as a society? And perhaps, most importantly, what can brown women be doing for themselves?

## A time and a place for appreciation

I often get asked when it is suitable for someone to share cultural aspects, or in other words, when is it OK for a white woman to wear a bindi? I'll give you a few examples. During my wedding festivities back in 2017, I wanted my white friends to feel as involved in the wedding process as everyone else. Before the wedding, my Melbourne-born bestie and I sat down over a coffee, and I explained the ins and outs of a Sikh wedding. I told her what would be going on during the lead-up to the main day, how she'll get to witness *haldi vatnaa* (turmeric powder and oil paste) being rubbed all over me at the *maiya*, the banter that will go down between my *nanke* (mum's side) and *dadke* (dad's side) at the ladies' *sangeet* when singing old folk songs, and we even spoke about the history of henna. Most importantly, I went through the meaning of the actual wedding ceremony, the Anand Karaj, and how important the union is, not only to us as a couple but also to our Guru. She sat and listened to every little detail for almost three hours. She even took notes. So, for her to wear a full Punjabi salwar kameez (she, in fact, borrowed my mum's, with her permission), sari, bangles and bindi to my wedding felt acceptable at that time and place. To be honest, she probably knew more about it all than most Punjabis attending the wedding. The point is, she did not make any assumptions about what she could and couldn't do. She took the time to listen and to learn. She did not take without permission.

When trying to figure out whether you're appropriating another culture or not, I found that writer Nisi Shawl's (2005) essay 'Appropriate Cultural Appropriation' (such a fitting title) was a handy guide. When it comes to a cultural symbiosis, we can usually fit the issues into three clear categories: 'guests', 'tourists' and 'invaders'. For example, a guest sharing cultural aspects is not too much of a problem – you could be two friends, often swapping clothes and learning from each other. As a guest, you would hope they'd want to learn and understand more about you and your culture. Casey, my Melbourne bestie, would be a good example of a 'guest'. A 'tourist' (in this context perhaps a white person visiting a South Asian country) can sometimes be a little irritating, but you give them a pass if they fall into acts of appropriation. They sometimes violate your area's 'house rules', but you hope they will come to be enlightened and learn about your culture. This is why backpackers and tourists can usually get a pass. Finally, there are the 'invaders' – someone who has deliberately invaded your space without warning, commodifying and profiteering from aspects of your culture without any regard for its history, context or how it might make people from that background feel. It makes no sense for the invader to be adopting that cultural accessory or object in the given context, time or place. So, if you're ever questioning whether you are appropriating something or not, see whether you fit into any of those three categories. If it's the latter, press pause and reassess.

We all need to be especially alert to things that are held sacred in other cultures. Sure, we have the right to express ourselves freely through the clothes that we wear, but can you see why wearing a T-shirt with a Hindu god or any religious deity or symbol might be a bit insensitive? Try to ask yourself some questions first. Here, I'd like to emphasize Susan Scafidi's three S's – 'Source, Significance, Similarity'. Think about the source community, who are they, what is their history? Do they perhaps have a background of exploitation, slavery or maybe even genocide? Does your participation benefit or hinder the community? Significance – is it a sacred object, what weight and meaning does it hold? How is it represented through the product, is it demeaned or made fun of? And finally, similarity – is it copying a cultural object or concept that originally belonged to another culture? If the answer to any of these questions is yes, you may hopefully have learnt why it may be offensive to the source community.

Larger institutions also have a role to play in this messy cultural appropriation world. The fact that basements of museums here in the UK are full of undisplayed, unstudied and unappreciated works of art from the South Asian continent is maddening to me. I'm not saying that all these items should come out onto exhibition floors or go back to the countries they were taken from (there's a long-standing debate on this), and I appreciate that collections and artifacts get rotated, but I do think museums and places of so-called heritage have a responsibility to portray an inclusive and accurate narrative of the role that ethnic minorities played in the history of this country. This means tackling touchy topics such as the contested legacy of the British Empire, racism and muted voices. By doing so, we can avoid nasty situations of cultural appropriation taking place.

Some museums and historical sites are making strides in righting these wrongs. Kensington Palace asked me to run a community project as part of their Victoria exhibition. They realized they couldn't talk about Victoria without discussing the atrocities that took place while she was Empress and the process of decolonization that subsequently took place. The community project allowed brown women from London to see up-close some of the exhibition pieces before they went on display and write poems about how they made them feel. They spoke of the collapse of existing empires, the famine, the death, the rebellions, the plunder, the fourteen million people displaced during partition. The poems were dark, sad and painful, but they went up on display alongside the exhibition's objects to show a more complex and nuanced picture of Victoria and her Empire. These opportunities allow women of colour to tell our stories from our own voices and to tell it in a way that we want to, rather than having others speak for us.

A lot of the issues we see within our current social and political climate are, in my view, related to Britain's history of not confronting and educating schoolchildren about the Empire appropriately. If our national curriculum included the injustices of the British Empire, as I highlighted in Chapter 2, and if we had an education system that included migration stories and voices from the South Asian continent during the decolonization period, perhaps this would reduce the amount of racial and cultural insensitivity that takes place in society. As always, education is the key.

What about a top-down approach? One of the problems with tackling cultural appropriation is that there is a lack of legal framework to address when cultural misappropriation takes place, especially by multinational corporations and businesses, which leaves communities without guidance or protection. There are laws against speeding, drug use and littering, and we know that these things are next to impossible to enforce. Yet the fact that these laws exist reinforces the idea that society disapproves of these activities, and they can act as a deterrent. If cultural appropriation was recognized as similarly harmful, the law would at least attempt to assign rights and set guidelines for behaviour. More significantly, the source community usually has relatively little political power or is otherwise outside of the mainstream culture and its political and legal frameworks. That means that lawmakers have little incentive to address the issue. So, we're back to square one. Again, the problem is that we need more brown women in positions of power who can use the mic to help voice their concerns. Whether it's representation in the political sphere, whether in boardrooms of businesses and companies, whether it's executive positions on boards and councils, we need brown women at the forefront of these conversations to call out the bullshit. To push for systems to be put in place when these issues of appropriation arise, and to fight for repercussions for when the appropriation is causing harm.

When I spoke to Preet Gill, MP for Edgbaston in Birmingham and the first female Sikh MP, about the importance of Asian women in politics representing our voice, she explained how crucial it was for her to use her voice to 'speak on issues that matter to my constituents and my community . . .' She went on to say that 'as legislators, what we say and how we say it makes a difference to all those female South Asian voices who don't see people like me on those green benches. Whether it's issues of hate crime, gender inequality or debating the NHS, I realize that my voice brings with it the richness of my experiences, background and values. I want to encourage more Asian women to enter politics, and they will only do that if they see women like me in that role.'

All these possible solutions take us back around to a similar thread. The public and private image of our communities are extremely important. Whether it's fictional portrayals or those in real life, meaningful representation of brown women will not only have a significant impact on our communities, but also help others to understand our culture, to not disrespect it or participate in its erasure. It means establishing ourselves, again, as the most important voices in protecting and portraying our own cultures.

When I was growing up, I wanted to abandon my culture so badly just because it never felt cool. Growing up in the nineties, Britney Spears, Christina Aguilera and the Spice Girls were all the rage; I'd see all the girls in music videos with short haircuts and miniskirts and I wanted to be like them and look like them so badly. But those were some Western cultural crazes I wasn't allowed to adopt. As I've got older and I look back at these moments, I don't mind so much that I didn't get to wear skirts or have short hair or do all the things that the white girls did. What I mind more is why I wanted so badly to fit in. Why, essentially, did I want to be white? One of the surest ways to conquer cultural appropriation, in fact, has got nothing to do with the white man – or the white woman. It's to do with understanding ourselves better, understanding and loving and respecting our own culture and identity before we expect others to.

I'm not saying we should love every part of our cultures. Some aspects of them can be misogynistic and contextually no longer viable – the ongoing preference for sons and stigma around menstruation being just two examples. But still, we need to feel confident in who we are and our place in the world for others not to walk over us. At the end of the day, a white person or celebrity can take off their make-up, bindi and jewellery, and reflect on what an amazing time they just had and how fit they looked. At the end of my day, I take off my make-up, bindi and jewellery, and I'm still going to be a brown girl, with all the difficulties and joys that brings. I could sulk and think about how much I missed out on as a kid. Or, instead, I can try and be more in love with who I am now.

# CHAPTER 7

# 'I WAS AT THE LIBRARY'

*Love, 'Dating' and Relationships*

*There were walls built around me, each brick concealing some shame*
*Each cement crease covering up a scar, a bruise, a secret, a name*
*My eyes were always tired, and my cheeks were always wet*
*But after being pushed so often, I had learnt to watch my step*
*You asked me if I was ready to be loved and I kept thinking, not yet*
*But then I realised I couldn't keep making you pay for someone else's debt*
*'What did they do that made you want to hate yourself so much?'*
*Why was I so scared to ask for help or flinched at someone's touch?*
*I told others to love themselves more, but couldn't take my own advice*
*Because deep down I thought I was nothing but an ocean made of ice*
*But one look at you and I melted, I eased into your palm*
*Because after years of panic and fear, I finally felt some calm*
*'How am I meant to hold your hand if it's always in a fist?'*
*I let go, I let myself free and greeted true love with a kiss*
*I told you that you have no choice but to love me like I'm art*
*Sell all your secrets and with the truth pay rent to live in my heart*
*You've made your roll, high as a kite, burning higher and higher*

*Because only a man like you was able to love a **girl made out of fire**.*

found this chapter the hardest to start. Maybe because it's the topic that scares me the most. It's the topic we've been writing about since ancient civilizations, through art, through music, through stories, through film. I've written hundreds of poems about it over the years, especially since I met my partner, Mr Indy Hothi. It's the one thing we can never stop talking about, and no matter how much we explore it and write about it, we still have no idea how to navigate it. Love. The word that either gives you hope for all humanity or makes you roll your eyes in disgust. I've felt both. I initially set out writing this book telling myself to write about what I know. But equally, I know I still have so much to learn. And I think that's the thing about love, we'll never know enough. I've spent months listening to the stories of other brown women on relationships, marriage, divorce, heartbreak and singlehood. And I still have no idea what to tell you. But there is one thing I do know; brown women know what love is. And we know what it is not.

I wrote and rewrote the subtitle to this chapter about ten times because even as a grown-ass woman, I felt like my mum might tell me off for even mentioning the word 'dating'. Because brown folks don't date. Well – we all know we do, but you know the sitch. You've got to tell everyone you were 'at the library' when you were really meeting that cute guy that sits behind you in Friday's lecture for a coffee. It's not that we want to lie, but when you've been taught to avoid boys like the plague your whole life, the conventions of love, relationships and dating can look a bit different. Most of us are told 'don't talk to boys, don't be friends with boys, stay away from boys' for the majority of our childhood and young adulthood. Then all of a sudden, there is a time post-university when we're in the prime of our twenties when something dramatic happens – as if the tectonic plates had suddenly shifted! And with it comes the tsunami of questions which include, almost aggressively, 'do you know any nice boys?' or 'you should be thinking about marriage.' Or better still, 'auntie from the temple knows a really nice boy for you.' Apparently, an expiry date that we were not aware of has been plastered onto our foreheads, sparkling in gold. But remember, 'It's your timeline, not society's timeline, not your family's timeline . . .' as Sonya Barlow, founder of the Like Minded Females network, tells me.

Which brings us to the question, is it harder for brown girls these days to find love, and to learn what love even means? Because we're already standing on rocky ground. Sheetal Mistry, co-founder of the community platform South Asian Sisters Speak (SASS), tells me, 'Yes and no. In many cases, women can now make their own decisions about who they want to date or marry, and families are slowly becoming more open-minded as to who their daughters are "allowed" to be with. But that last part – about who we're "allowed" to be with – is still a problem. I know myself and my friends consciously approach dating by thinking within the parameters of who our families will accept – there's still a limit, even though we are hypothetically allowed to choose for ourselves.'

Pearly Pouponneau, the host of *The Diatribe Podcast*, says she sympathizes with the current generation of brown women in the dating field. 'You're damned if you do and you're damned if you don't!' she says. 'We always have to answer to the South Asian community no matter what path we choose. Whether you're choosing to be single, whether you are single and want to be in a relationship, whether you're exploring the dating field or whether you're just talking to a couple of different people – no matter what, a brown woman always feels she has to answer to somebody, and even if you don't feel that pressure, it's still very much there. The community expects so much of brown women.'

## The multiple forms of love

At the start of this book, you may remember that I spoke about the importance of not letting others define who we are. The same can be applied to the brown love story. It's up to us to write it for ourselves. So where does this brown love story begin?

For brown folk in the Western world, the love we see and learn around us is often as confusing and conflicting as it is for anyone else. We grew up watching films and listening to music about affection, kissing, hugging, chocolates and flowers. These typically 'romantic' representations of love often conflicted with what we saw in our own homes. That kind of affection was definitely not going on in my house! We'd even change the channel if it looked like someone was about to kiss on *EastEnders*! But over the years, I began to learn that the love I saw in my home wasn't more or less valid than these other interpretations of love. It was just different. My mum and dad have been married for over forty years. They have always looked after each other. My dad may not have showered my mum with chocolates and flowers on the last Valentine's Day, but a week or so later, he bought her a bin liner filled with a year's supply of her favourite Olay cream because it was on sale. To me, that's also love.

We all know that the kind of love we see in Hollywood movies, or Bollywood and *Star Plus* dramas isn't real life but we still all aspire to the dream. But brown girls are subjected to an extra pressure, often wrapped up in thick layers of capitalist patriarchy, that tells brown women that their only goal in life is their wedding day. I know girls who have planned every single detail of their wedding, from their outfit to the centrepieces. They've even got a date set. Only one problem – they are still waiting on a groom. There is no problem with dreaming about your wedding day, but in the words of activist and writer Amrit Wilson, I don't want any girl to feel that it's her *only* 'pinnacle of glory and her raison d'être'. I promised myself I'd keep this chapter as light-hearted as possible, but the capitalism, objectification and commercialization going on in brown weddings – specifically for the bride – is harmful. Society teaches brown girls to grow up dreaming of their wedding, not about their life. Imagine if we, as brown families, saved as much money to invest in our daughters' studies, ideas, and business ventures, as we do in their big blow-out wedding receptions. Imagine if we supported their other dreams, too. Priya Mulji, a senior columnist at the *Eastern Eye*, has been there. 'People will ask about my love life before they ask about my writing achievements. Not to toot my own horn here, but isn't it amazing that I write a column for a national newspaper?' It is amazing, Priya! And you have every right to toot your own horn. If we first stop treating a wedding as a brown woman's only achievement, maybe it would give her a chance to learn for herself what love actually means.

I don't want to give the impression that love is a scarcity, when in fact, it's in abundance. Love exists. Love is radical. Love is gentle. Love is hard. Love heals. It is here that I'd also like to emphasize that love doesn't necessarily mean finding 'the one'. Many women are rejecting the notion that their life is incomplete and they will have failed unless they find 'the one'. To think that way is not love. I have wonderful friends who have decided to remain single, some that are single parents, some that have to look after their parents in their old age. To me, that kind of love is equally important, valid and special as finding a partner. Don't let those tropes lessen your version of love. Your definition of love, the skills of love, both giving and receiving, is ultimately yours to form.

Often, we get so wrapped up in this idea of finding the right partner that we don't spend enough time learning our love languages: what does love look like and feel like to you? And have you ever taken the time to consider how the people around you wish to be loved? Because everyone speaks a different love language, and we're only going to become effective communicators of love if we take time to learn it. Pearly, who we met earlier in the chapter, put it perfectly – 'It's one thing to tell somebody you love them but are you loving them the way they need to be loved?'

Knowing your love language is damn sexy. When I see or meet women who either know and/or are learning what they need in love, I'm drooling. But like anything worthwhile, it takes time to learn, and this learning can happen in all kinds of places. Writer and mother Anmol Merban tells me that she had to consider her love language for the first time in front of her whole family! Her father had found her a potential match, and after the 'formal' family meetings, it was Anmol's turn to meet him. 'We met with the addition of fifteen family members. Fifteen!' she tells me. After the initial formalities, Anmol and Mr 'Great Black Leather Jacket' as she called him, finally had a chance to ask each other a few questions. She tells me: 'This man leaned forward, resting his elbows on his knee and says: "What are you looking for in a partner?" The crowd roared with cheer, amazement and shock . . . The family members were all salivating and bouncing their eyes back and forth when we spoke to each other or when we didn't speak, everyone there was just observing us under a microscope!' I asked Anmol what she said back. 'I did finally say "respect", and he agreed and gave me a warm nod (I kind-of blushed).' Anmol and her partner have been happily married since 2017. They continued to learn their love languages through their early years of marriage. When she was completing her dissertation for her degree, which was due one day before her baby's delivery date, she says her partner gave her all the 'words of affirmation' that she needed. 'I had to pull my big pregnancy pants up and get on with it . . . My partner gave me non-stop reassurance, support and encouragement.' Here, Anmol has described one of the five emotional love languages by author and relationship counsellor Gary Chapman. These include quality time, acts of service, touch, gifts and, as for Anmol, words of affirmation. Each of us has a hierarchy of which of these languages we prefer more than others. For those that need words of affirmation, a verbal compliment or kind and encouraging words can go a long way. I feel that.

When Mr Indy Hothi and I first got together, he assumed one of my love languages was gifts, as this may have been a language he'd learnt in the past. He'd buy me fancy presents and take me to dinners in Michelin-starred restaurants, but as lovely as they were, neither of us were that fulfilled by them. However, when he took me to Comicon for the first time or when we took my nephews and niece to Planet Hollywood, we were smiling ear to ear! We realized it wasn't about spending a load of money, we both just loved quality time with each other. In a world with so many distractions, we just wanted to be present in love. It was one of the most important aspects of our love language hierarchy. It's one of the main reasons we decided to take a year out and go on a twelve-month backpacking trip across Asia and Africa for our honeymoon. We didn't want a big fat Indian wedding, so instead, we put a deposit down for our first home and built memories of quality time around the globe! Our quality time now includes long dog walks, eating yummy street food, working out together, more travelling, and exploring our passions like arts and culture.

In fact, our shared love of arts was precisely what led us to meeting each other in the first place! He was in the audience at my very first poetry performance. After years of writing poetry, I finally plucked up the courage to perform at an arts event taking place over in west London. Being born and raised on the east side, I convinced myself that I wouldn't know anyone there, so if the performance was a complete train wreck, I could run back home and never do it again. I had nothing to lose. In the audience that night was my now husband. Indy was there scouting for poets to perform at an upcoming exhibition he was holding in the city. I thank God every day for introducing me to two loves that night. My love for spoken word poetry and the love of my life. I wouldn't be where I am today and I certainly wouldn't be here now, writing this book, without the two of them.

Touch is also one of my top three love languages. A warm cuddle and a cup of tea can literally fill up my love tank. Indy calls it my sunshine, my fuel, what I need to keep growing. Cuddles, hugs and kisses amongst other forms of touch that are not PG13 enough for this book, keep me alive. Charmaine Gandhi, who recently graduated from the University of Bath as a Politics and International Relations student, tells me that 'physical affection or words of affirmation were never really a thing between them [her parents].' She hopes this is something that she can unlearn, as it may be one of her love languages. She wants to explore this more with her current partner.

I guess this is where we should address the elephant in the room . . . Let's talk about sex. I know it's the conversation that most brown families avoid like the plague. But we have to. And I'm afraid I'm not going to dive into the saucy details about what Indy and I get up to after hours. But I do want to emphasize that brown women should be able to make choices about their body without feeling guilty or ashamed. There are many misconceptions about brown women and sex, such as, brown women don't do it (lol). But popular podcasts like *Masala Podcast* and *Brown Girls Do It Too* are tackling the misconceptions and shame through honest conversations about sex – the good, the bad and the ugly! It's a physical love language in its rawest form.

We all have a hierarchy as to which of the five qualities is more important to us than others, and this is often something that brown girls don't get to communicate with their partners. While a head massage after a long day at work might make someone who values physical touch feel like a million pounds, the same gesture may not mean all that much to someone else. So often we try and give people what *we* want. Sometimes it's about listening and learning, sometimes it takes a bit of trial and error. And that's OK. In her stunning book *See No Stranger*, Valarie Kaur says that 'Love is a form of sweet *labor*: fierce, bloody, imperfect, and life-giving – a choice we make over and over again. Love can be taught, modelled, and practiced.' If Valarie is right, and if love is a type of labour, then isn't it about time we learnt about it? Because even love can sometimes get lost in translation when we're all speaking different love languages. But once we speak these languages to each other, we feel heard, we feel validated, we feel loved. And this can be applied to any relationship.

It's through this love-language-self-discovery-expedition (wow that was a mouthful) that we begin to recognize what kinds of behaviours we should and should not accept from others within the realms of love. Because I know I have had a serious problem in this realm. I made a self-diagnosis a few years ago. I suffer from a people-pleaser-problem.* They call me a yes-man because I can't seem to say 'no'. I take on way too many jobs for other people, I put my own desires last. And guess what? Brown women are the ultimate people-pleasers. Yeah – I said it. Remember when I said we were the ultimate code-switchers in Chapter 2? Well with that heavyweight title also comes the heavier burden of always wanting to please people. What comes with the skill of being able to morph and mould ourselves in any surrounding – whether that's at work, at home with the kids, with the in-laws at the weekend or chatting to auntie at your cousin's sangeet night – is the need to people-please. It's been a part of our survival mechanism for so long. It was our only way to exist.

* [*people-pleaser-problem*, noun; an illness where you can't say no to others]

187

Freelance writer and author of the popular blog *Mani's Madness*, Mani Hayre, wrote that 'ever since I was a child I have been a complete and utter people pleaser, always fearing that I was doing something wrong [. . .] So in my early 20s not wanting to amount to much [. . .] I went to India and was engaged when I got back three weeks later. At the time, it seemed like the right thing to do, this was my "people pleasing" phase.' The marriage ended a very long time ago, and Mani is in a much better place, but even at thirty-seven, she is still unlearning. It's never too late to learn where our 'nos' and our boundaries lie. *The Diatribe Podcast* host, Pearly, told me that 'it took me twenty-seven years to learn what the word boundaries even meant. It's OK to say no.' When we choose to people-please, we decide to chip away at ourselves and spread ourselves too thinly, so thinly that we actively silence parts of ourselves. It's important we stay whole and full, and not settle for crumbs from people. Otherwise, we will always be hungry, and we'll always be put last. You shouldn't have to earn people's love by trying to please them all the time. This kind of people-pleasing is rooted in fear. But we, as brown women, can no longer keep people-pleasing if it is to the detriment of ourselves. Never mind how exhausting it is. Take the wheel. Say no when you need to, set your boundaries, don't settle for little crumbs, eat the whole cake, and stay full.

## The quest for love

I appreciate that it's not always that simple. If it were, I wouldn't need to write this book! And once brown women have climbed aboard the love-language-self-discovery-boundary-setting-expedition train, the next question appears . . . How do I

188

*actually* meet a guy these days? This seems to be a common question amongst most of my single girlfriends. And I guess there is no simple answer. Whether it's meeting someone online, whether it's arranged, whether you've met him at work, whether you've known him from school – who really cares! For years, I've seen the mainstream representation of brown relationships and marriages follow the same old lousy and lazy storylines of 'backwards arranged marriages' and 'poor passive housewives'. It was easy for the Western media to point fingers East when it came to the patriarchal traditions of marriage, yet it was only as recently as 1991 that the UK classified rape in marriage as rape. My point is, it's not about which culture is more archaic than the other, it's that we need to be telling the brown love story with our own voices. Otherwise, we're going to keep seeing these sad sorry-ass narratives time and time again. And telling stories doesn't always have to be through books, TV and movies. We can tell our love stories by *actually* modelling them. Anmol, who we heard from earlier, is an example of a healthy arranged marriage. 'There has been a misconception of arranged marriages, and I truly feel honoured that I'm able to reshape what it means. In the twenty-first century it means mutual agreement from both parties,' she told me. She too was anti arranged marriages for some time, but found that it worked perfectly for her. Don't get me wrong, we all know there are many horror stories when it comes to arranged marriages, but it's important that we hear the beautiful stories too.

There are those who have found love through the digital world. There are apps, networks, sliding into DMs, dropping cheeky emails – Shakespeare's Sonnets ain't got nothing on Sanjay's selfies! Former French translator turned digital marketer

Seetal Salva tells me an email reignited her movie-worthy love story. She met her now-husband during her first year at university when a mutual friend introduced them. 'Things changed after graduation when he went travelling, and I moved to Montreal. One day, when he was going through his email contacts, he hovered over my name and contemplated deleting my details. Instead, he emailed me, and we reconnected . . .' said Seetal.

'Our first kiss took place in a bar next to the Moulin Rouge, lights flashing, music blaring and drinks flowing. We've just celebrated our twelfth anniversary. Très Bollywood, right?' *Oui oui*, Seetal! But just like the horror stories of arranged marriages, the digital world does not come without its own warnings, or you might be on the receiving end of catfishing, privacy violations or an unsolicited dick pic or two. Yousra Imran, the author of *Hijab and Red Lipstick*, told me about her interesting online dating experience . . . 'On one date in a busy cafe, the guy happened to be a professional singer. I'm not easily fazed by guys, especially when they're trying hard to impress, so I was like "oh, that's cool." Next thing I know, he breaks out into full song and performs an entire song right there in front of everyone. Literally, everyone turned around, some a bit dazed and others amused. He was trying to maintain eye contact the whole time, but I couldn't meet his eye! I wanted the ground to swallow me up!' Despite this hilarious and presumably awkward experience, Yousra didn't lose hope. 'It was fourth-time lucky on the app' when she connected with her husband. 'We had our nikah, the Islamic marriage ceremony, two months later and we've now been happily married for three years.' If Anmol's, Seetal's or Yousra's examples tell us anything, it's that we can find love in all kinds of ways and that everyone's timeline is different!

I recognize that many of the stories and thoughts we've heard so far are heterosexual, cis-gendered examples. We still have a long way to go in our communities if we are to provide an open and healthy space to talk about our gay, lesbian, bisexual or trans experiences of love and relationships. Homosexuality was only decriminalized in India in 2018 with the scrapping of Section 377, which criminalized 'carnal intercourse against the order of nature with any man, woman or animal'.

But despite what governments are or are not doing, despite the whispers at family functions, despite how the media does or does not represent queer love, I'm overjoyed to see it blooming, breaking barriers and existing more openly than ever before. Incredible organizations like Gaysians, the umbrella brand for the South Asian LGBTQ+ community, have been doing incredible work to ensure that the experiences of love and relationships from a non-heterosexual brown voice are also reaching the mainstream. Gaysians has built a network of over twenty-four different LGBTQ+ organisations, including Hidayah, who provide guidance for the Muslim community, and Sarbat, a volunteer-led group addressing LGBTQ+ issues from a Sikh perspective. There's also Dosti, a social and support group for South Asian and Middle Eastern LGBTQ+ people, which meets every month and provides online support groups.

This support, solidarity and visibility is a vital part of the brown love story. Someone who knows the importance of queer visibility all too well is Saima Razzaq, activist and chair of SEEDS (Supporting Education of Equality and Diversity in

Schools). Saima was the first gay Muslim woman to lead Pride in 2019. She told me how it was 'a really powerful moment. I wanted to present myself authentically, so I decided to don myself in my favourite Pakistani suit and bangles. I will never throw my community under the bus and label them all homophobes because that simply is not the case. By presenting myself authentically, I am bringing more and more people with me on this journey of equality.'

Over the years, I've lost friends and family members for speaking in defence of LGBTQ+ and queer love in general, often fighting those who consider themselves the most pious and loving people. I tell them that they can't know what love really is if they can't accept all love. I've had religious texts quoted at me as a justification for their homophobia. The irony here is that I lean into my faith to learn true *pyaar* (love). To live with *sat* (truth) and to let others live their truth, to live with *daya* (compassion) and live empathetically, in the hope that we all find our *santokh* (contentment) in this world. Now that's love.

Trainee psychologist Monica Nakra tells me she met her partner through faith at a kirtan programme at the Gurdwara. 'We connected through Sikhi and similar mindsets . . .' she says. 'My bibi (grandma) always said "jithe sanjog lika aa uthe hona aa", meaning "wherever it is written, that is where it will happen"!' Perhaps Monica's bibi is on to something. In the Sikh faith, this is known as 'Divine Will' or *Hukam*, becoming in harmony with the will of God. Whether you believe in God or not, the value here is allowing yourself to have some peace, knowing whatever is meant to be will be. If the benefit of leaning into the teachings of our elders or our faith brings us more peace and more wellbeing inside, then don't push it away. Not all that our elders have to teach us about love is outdated. If anything, we need to hold some of those teachings dear and close to our hearts. Their life experiences and all that they have seen would have taught them so much about love.

## Timeless love

I love listening to the golden nuggets of wisdom that Beeji gives me. Beeji, Mohinder Kaur, is my husband's maternal grand-mother and pretty much raised him growing up. Usually, we would call a maternal grandmother Naniji, but Indy and his family have called her Beeji for as long as they can remember. It is a name often given to mothers or grandmothers out of endearment. When a video of Beeji which I posted on Twitter went viral, I realized lots of communities other than the Sikh Punjabi one use this name too, including the East African and Pakistani communities. The video, which received around 60,000 views overnight, was of Beeji individually washing, drying and packing grapes for me to take to work the next day. The kindness and love put into this beautiful gesture speaks a thousand words. I talk about her a lot online. If you simply type 'Jaspreet Kaur Beeji' into a Google search engine, you will see all our posts. I frequently get asked what it's like to be living with my grandma-in-law (in-law talk being one of the hottest topics in the brown community), and I often say Beeji is the soulmate I never knew I needed. She and I sometimes joke that we must have met in another life because we have a very special 'connec-tion', in her words. She has taught me the true meaning of unconditional love. She has taught me that 'pyaar naal pathar

vee badaliaa ja sakadaa hai', meaning, 'even stone can be soft-
ened with a bit of love'. Beeji is what makes our house feel like a
home. When I interviewed Sonya, who I mentioned at the start
of the chapter, she said, 'In-laws aren't replacing your own
family. They are an extension of your own family.' And all the
emotional effort shouldn't be left to the 'daughter-in-law'. If
healthy family dynamics are to work after marriage, then everyone needs to be putting in the effort to communicate, to care and
to love, not just the new bride.

Indy's beeji reminds me a lot of my own late maternal
grandmother, Surjit Kaur, who we also called Beeji growing
up, a mother to all. But these two women have more in
common than just their pet name. They both became widows
at a young age. My grandma, Surjit Kaur (henceforth Beeji S
to save you from confusion), was born around 1936. Due to
the lack of official records and documentation in Punjab at the
time, we are not entirely sure of her official birth date.* Everyone who met her was astounded by her intelligence, strength,
humility, and pure heart. Not once would you ever hear her
utter hateful words to anyone; she could only speak words of
kindness. But, unfortunately, fate did not treat her with the
same consideration.

When she was of age, her marriage was arranged with my
nanaji, Kundan Singh. They were blessed with two children: my
beautiful mother and my uncle. However, when my mother was
only two and a half, her father died. Beeji S lost her husband,
and my mother and uncle lost their father far too soon. The

---

* Shoutout to all the grandparents whose passports say they're born on 1
January (if you know, you know . . .)

years that followed were difficult. As a widow, she was perceived as an extra mouth to feed. Much to the disbelief of those in the *pind*, Beeji S continued to work hard on the family land, completing all the manual labour, building and ploughing by herself. She wanted to make sure her children were educated and would not have to face the same hardships as she had. My mum tells me stories of how Beeji S would wake her and my uncle before sunrise with a lantern, and make them read and write before they went to school every morning. Against the will of others in the family, she made sure my mum carried on with her schooling. Family members said that my mother should be kept in the home, undertaking activities more suited to her gender, such as sewing or cooking. Yet my beeji S held her ground and said, 'If my daughter wants to study, then she will.' Thanks to my beeji S, my mum was one of the few women in the *pind* to go to college. Despite the hardship she endured for almost fifty years as a widow, Beeji S ultimately received the utmost respect from members of her village.

Widows like Beeji and Beeji S are so often betrayed by their state and their own communities, and sometimes their own families. There was a time where women like them would be burnt alongside their husband's funeral pyres. Yet I'm astounded that they were still able to show others nothing but love and lived in *chardi kala*, eternal optimism. Always kind, always smiling, always warm. Both women are as strong as steel but as gentle as a feather. People now speak of them both with such respect and admiration, you would think they were some sort of war veterans. And actually, the injustice that they had to endure for years was tantamount to war. But they survived. My gentle warriors . . . So, when Beeji now teaches me lessons on love and kindness, I want to soak up all that wisdom. It reminded me of an old proverb, 'Nawa Nau Din, Purana Sau Din', that means 'new for nine days, old for a hundred days'. It's OK to adopt new ways of thinking, but ancient wisdom can last and live with us in love too.

## Making myself smaller

When my late paternal grandad, Babaji, and the rest of my family went to meet Indy for the first time, I was terrified. Traditionally, when the bride's family visits the groom's family for the first time, the bride doesn't attend, so I was waiting at home shaking in my boots (aka, fluffy slippers!). Deep down, I knew they would all adore him, but my babaji was a very headstrong man, and his opinion mattered to me a lot. I waited. I texted my sister to ask her how it was going. She replied, 'We'll talk when we get home.' Shit . . . Did it not go well? Did Indy say something stupid?

When they arrived home, I remember standing at my living room window, peeping through the curtain to see the expressions on their faces as they all got out of the car. They were all beaming! My sister was just being a git to wind me up! When I asked my babaji what he thought of him, he said, 'He sits up very straight. Good posture.' That's it. No feedback on Indy's personality or his terrible banter, just his posture! To my babaji, this spoke a thousand words, this was a sign of a well-raised man. He did ask me one question though . . . 'Do you mind that he is shorter than you?' he asked. 'No, not at all,' I replied. To be completely honest, up until this point, it never occurred to me that Indy was two inches shorter than me. And I began to wonder why my grandad even asked me this question in the first place. It reminded me of times when my height had been a problem for brown men.

I think it was less about my long legs and more about how my height made them feel. Smaller? Less masculine, maybe? It reminded me of those many years when I tried to make myself smaller, both physically and metaphorically, because I felt 'too much'. Too tall. Too curvy. Too opinionated. Too political. Too anticipatory. Too intelligent. Too bright. Too much of myself. And every single time, I had to unfold my halved body, and my quartered mind and stand up whole again. Because it was never my job to mend fragile male egos, just as it is no one's job to make me feel like a woman. If your manhood is defined by how much richer, taller or stronger you are than your woman, then you've got a whole lot you need to unpack in therapy. Indy often gets asked by other men how he feels about me being taller than him, how he feels about my successes and ambitions, about me being on stage in front of large audiences . . . His answer: 'I couldn't be prouder. If anything, I want her to do more!' And with regards to my height? 'Well, we're all the same height lying down.' Cheeky!

These questions from brown men are usually rooted in their own insecurities, toxic masculinity and fragility. Mani Hayre says there are 'too many mummy's boys that feel threatened by strong independent women. They like the idea of us, even date us for a short amount of time, but in the long-term, I think it's not the ideal for them.' Shirin Shah, the fellow co-founder of SASS, expresses similar feelings. 'I think that a lot of men, for lack of a better word, the "woke ones", are really attracted to women who have everything going for them, with ambitions, side hustles and other interests beneath the surface . . . But as time goes on, and ultimately when the two paths clash, women are expected to be the ones to compromise and are asked to lessen their dreams.' Pharmacist Nimrata Gujral told me she had experienced this first-hand. 'I think many men still want to feel like the breadwinner and challenges to this cause conflict. In my previous marriage, my husband frequently told me that my job was not very good and that I wasn't very good at it. If I did apply for any new job or promotion, he told me I wouldn't get it. On one occasion I did get a large promotion, and he said that I should just think of it as good interview practice, as it wouldn't work with his long-term plans, and that I should decline the role.'

Somewhere along the line, some brown boys develop an understanding of love and relationships that seems to be about catering solely to their needs and plans. Does this come from childhood? Alya Mooro, journalist and bestselling author of *The Greater Freedom*, tells me that 'the way we raise our sons to be so pampered and looked after – "Habibi, what do you need? What can I get you?" – they come to expect that from all the women in their lives moving forward.' I agree with Alya, a lot of these issues stem from deep within our childhood socialization, and we will be tackling how we can do better in raising our brown babies in Chapter 8. With our full-time jobs, side hustles, multiple side hustles, volunteering, community organizing and code-switching into every shape and form, are we still expected to do ALL the domestic work, i.e. the second shift. This is not only patriarchal nonsense, it's also unrealistic. No one is saying we're *never* going to make you roti from time to time, so chill, we're just saying the load should be equally carried. And we hope our partners can support our dreams in the way that we hope to support theirs, and then communicate how those dreams look together, as a team.

## Truth telling

I do feel sorry for brown men. I know that it's the structures of patriarchy and hyper-masculinity that cause them to behave this way and prevent them from really exploring their emotions and speaking their truth. One day, I hope our empathy for one another helps us build healthier relationships. I hope brown men become more empathetic to the complexities that come with navigating the world in a brown woman's body, and on that same thread, men themselves start exploring where their feelings of insecurity, fragility and lack of fulfilment might be coming from. This will take time, patience, listening and learning. It will come when we can communicate honestly with one another. As with any relationship, healthy, clear communication is key. Most arguments, disagreements and misunderstandings arise from a lack of it. When we're busy making assumptions in our own heads rather than communicating with one another about how we feel, those emotions get bottled up and eventually turn into resentment. That resentment will come out at another time, in another argument, quite often over something relatively trivial, like leaving dirty socks on the floor. So, let's be honest. Let's be vulnerable. This requires *really* hearing the other person, whether it's the good, the bad or the ugly. Indy knows my deepest, darkest, scariest truths, ones that I thought I could never share. Through this kind of communication, we can build trust, one of the cornerstones to any relationship, and learn each other's love language. Building from a place of trust allows us to be willing to hear and speak our own truths. Don't get me wrong, I've had my trust broken a fair few times in the past. I have found out truths that cut real deep. But I no longer hold hate or pain there. I didn't want to hold any more space in me for that. It was literally a waste of space! So I have forgiven all the wrongs done to me and hope the same can go for any wrongs that I've done.

And we should never punish each other for speaking our truths, even if they hurt. This is what affirms the value of truth-telling and sets a foundation of trust, and sometimes the truth hurts and relationships have to end. In other cases, it's a foundation that love will hopefully grow from.

One of the ways to build this foundation of trust is through friendship. Can that person be your friend? Often, when brown girls are taught that the only reason for a relationship with a guy is getting married, they miss the great opportunity to find a friend in their partner. Pearly put it beautifully, she told me that she and her partner 'built a solid friendship before we entered an intimate partnership. I think that's one of the building blocks of a relationship, having a friendship first, respecting that person as a human being before loving and respecting them for being your partner.' Energy manager and mechanical engineer Jaz Rabadia MBE told me, 'For two years, Dips and I were in the "friend zone" before we eventually sealed the deal with a kiss. You see, I had to be sure that we were truly compatible, that we were spiritually aligned and that we had complementing life goals. In those two years, we became the very best of friends, we flirted, we introduced each other to our innermost friend circles, and we even wrote cute little notes to one another on strips of receipt roll, to pass the time on our shifts at work.' Jaz tells me that she and Dips met whilst working part-time student jobs in Sainsbury's, jokingly quoting Rihanna's *We Found Love*!

I think it really helps to see the other individual in their natural environment and – at risk of sounding like David Attenborough – in the wild! Observe what they are like in their own spaces, around their friends, around their family. This is especially important for brown girls who are introduced to someone they don't know well enough already. Tan, a secondary school maths teacher, told me that seeing her now-husband in his natural environment is what made her fall in love with him. Initially, she and her family had rejected the *rishta*. She thought he wasn't her type. She told me: 'On the Monday after half term, I started my new job in a school and guess who else works there . . .' What an awkward first day! 'Over the next few weeks, we both got on really well. The more time I spent with him, the more amazing I found him and the more I fell in love with him. A few months later, he told me he loved me. We told our parents within the week that we wanted to get married.' Tan and her husband have now been married for over seven years and have two beautiful children.

Before I asked Indy to marry me (yes, I asked him to marry me – we'll come back to that in a moment!) I observed him in the wild. I attended the events he was holding in the city in the Diversity & Inclusiveness space. I went to all the art exhibitions he held. I saw that he treated the waiting staff at restaurants with kindness and respect, was never rude, demanding or dismissive. In his spaces, he was always empathetic, always cheeky! A cool confidence I couldn't get enough of. He carried himself with the most gorgeous mixture of dignity and poise, but also spontaneity and silliness. And after two months of observing and really getting to know each other, I asked him to marry me. He was everything I wanted and never knew I needed, and I wanted to spend the rest of my life with him. He observed me in my spaces too, he came to all my shows, hung out with my family and me and picked me up from school when I was teaching. Sometimes, going on a 'first date' can feel so much like being at a job interview, you forget entirely how to be the real you! You've come prepared with the best questions, you're wearing your best outfit, hair looking real good, you answer all the questions to the best of your ability because you think that's what the other person wants to hear. Whereas seeing each other over time in our natural environments allows us to be our most authentic selves. Indy learnt that I get grouchy as hell when I'm hungry, I hate the cold, I'm sensitive and I cry a lot, but I'm strong as fuck. He knew I wouldn't stop fighting for the things I cared about even if it killed me. He saw every version of me, and by that point, I was so honest with myself about who I was that I didn't really care if anyone else liked it or not.

## Self-love is the starting place

Shortly before Indy and I got together, I had spent around twelve months on the love-language-self-discovery-boundary-setting-expedition train that I told you about earlier. I spent much of that time single, discovering myself. Accepting myself. And it was here that I built the very necessary foundation for self-love. I came to understand that this foundation of self-love, just like the foundation of a house, must be strong, because it is on this foundation that the other rooms of love can be built. Only then can you start filling the rooms with the love of others. For many of us, this foundation of self-love may have been broken down. This may be due to witnessing unhealthy relationships in our childhood or in our homes. It could have been due to a toxic boyfriend, or being bullied. Our self-love foundation has instead been replaced with quicksand, and anything we try to place on top of it would fall into an abyss. But it's never too late to start building your strong foundation of self-love.

Anmol found her self-love when she had her first child, which goes to show it can happen at any point in life: 'As clichéd as this will sound, I found me through my son [. . .] The only way I could teach love and happiness to my son was by also learning to prioritize myself.' Before that, she said she was in the 'deep sorrow of trying to find someone to love me the way I should have loved myself.' Suneeta Kaur Seera (Ceese), who works in the police force and has an awesome blog called *Say It How It Is,* told me she didn't know what self-love was until she was truly broken after her first marriage. 'I hated the way I looked and barely could look at myself in the mirror. I had to learn to heal. That's when I realized more about myself [. . .] Relationships come and go, but the relationship you have with yourself lives forever.' Of course, most of what I'm saying here applies to all women, in all types of relationships.

There is a self-assertiveness that comes with self-love. I developed a willingness to stand up for myself. As someone who doesn't like conflict and, as you've learnt already, a people-pleaser, this was hard. But if I wanted to have more meaningful and healthy encounters in my relationships, romantic or other-wise, I needed to hold my ground on the things I really cared about. Setting boundaries. Saying no, in order to say yes to myself.

We cannot control how others decide to love us, but we can choose how we love ourselves. I do believe this can be particularly hard for brown girls. Our parents, who had their own struggles and were often forging very difficult lives for themselves, as I explored earlier, don't always bring us up to feel like this. The idea of self-love probably isn't a priority, when you are fighting just to make a decent life for yourself and your children. But once we love ourselves, we can decide which love we accept. I have always said that the best leaders lead by example, and the same can be applied to love. Lead by example, love yourself in the way you wish others to love you. Show up for yourself! Manifestation is real, my friends! Manifesting is fostering the experience of what it is that you want to feel – and then living and believing in that experience so that you can allow it to come into form. I was filling myself up so much on self-love, I stopped accepting crumbs and started eating the whole damn cake. I was able to look at myself in the mirror and say – yes, I'll go to bed with you every night! To love yourself does not make you selfish. It does not make you narcissistic. If anything, a full tank of self-love gives you extra fuel to be more loving, more giving, more empathetic, more compassionate. Centring ourselves does not make us self-centred.

Self-love is about more than putting on a mask – and it can't be bought or sold. I know there is a growing industry focused on profiting off self-love and self-care and, don't get me wrong, I'm all for a #selfcaresunday, or what I prefer to call 'hair-wash-Sunday'. But remember that these are short-term validations that should be built into a broader toolkit of loving ourselves. Celebrating ourselves. By doing this, we continue to move into spaces that celebrate us. It is here that we can create a culture where love can flourish. It is here that I found a celebration of my brown identity. It was here that I formed a room of love for the brown sisterhood. It is here that we can find more love and empathy for others.

I now always treat this foundation of self-love and my rooms full of love with tenderness, kindness and care. To me, love should feel like a sacred place. There is a beautiful quote in John Welwood's book *Love and Awakening*, which says, 'When we reveal ourselves to our partner and find that this brings healing rather than harm, we make an important discovery – that intimate relationship can provide a sanctuary from the world of façades, a sacred space where we can be ourselves, as we are . . .' More recently, Justin Bieber put his own interpretation on this in the song 'Holy' – listen to the lyrics and you'll see what I mean. By speaking our individual love languages, by telling our truths and by loving ourselves, we find a very special, safe and sacred place in our rooms for love. Protect those rooms and take time to nourish them. A brown woman is filled with many rooms of love and, sometimes, the people who we meet through our lives will have keys to these rooms. Others, they come with hammers. Choose your people wisely.

# CHAPTER 8

# MUM'S THE WORD

*Parenthood and Raising a Brown Feminist*

*How are we meant to stay silent?*
*When even our birth*
*Is an act of rebellion*

'It's a girl . . .' For years, I wondered why these three simple words have such power to terrify parents, shatter communities, and even shake up entire countries. My anger and confusion led me to write a whole thesis on it for my postgraduate degree in gender studies. But it also led me to one of the most heartbreaking stories that my grandad ever told me. The story I am about to tell you might come as a shock for some, but for others, it will reaffirm everything we already know and feel about violence towards women and girls . . .

We were sitting in our living room one evening, Babaji reading the most recent copy of the *Des Pardes* newspaper whilst still managing to have one ear on the radio, me reading books on post-colonial theories on gender – you know, just some light reading. He asked what I was studying so intently, and I began to tell him about my research on female infanticide in Punjab. He seemed sincerely interested . . . then suddenly he went quiet and still, as if he had frozen in his seat. Babaji was so often the life of the party and the loudest voice in any room, so this wasn't normal. I saw his eyes drift off into the distance. I could tell from the expression on his face that his mind had gone somewhere dark. After a few moments of silence, he began to tell the story of one of his elder relatives who had two daughters, aged five and seven. One day, the father woke the two daughters and told them to get dressed in their best clothes and get ready to leave. He was

209

going to take them on a trip to Goindwal Gurdwara, a Gurdwara well known in Punjab for its *baoli* (stepwell), paved with eighty-four steps. With pure excitement, the two girls quickly got ready, and they set off on their journey. After some time walking, they eventually reached a long dirt road alongside a river. Hand in hand, the two girls happily skipped down the road.

Suddenly, and without any hesitation, the father pushed the two girls into the river. Neither of them was able to swim, and they both drowned. The father continued on to the Gurdwara, sat there and relaxed as if nothing had happened. When he returned home later that day, he said to the family, 'The deed was done.' Babaji paused at this point. He looked at my face, my eyes filled with tears. 'Are you sure you want to hear any more?' he asked. 'Yes . . .' I replied, hesitantly.

He then gave me another example of a Hindu family from a nearby village. A woman had been pregnant, and the family waited anxiously for the birth. The child was born, and with the realization that it was a baby girl, Babaji told me the mother suffocated the baby to death. They then dug a ditch at the back of their farm and stuffed her body in. Soon afterwards, dogs dug out the body and consumed it . . .

I ran out of the living room and into the bathroom, retching over the sink. I couldn't hear any more. Researching theories, policies and interventions about gender-based violence was one thing, but hearing these stories first-hand shook me to my core. And it was all down to son preference – to entrenched gender inequality. Because apart from anything else, sons are seen to provide financial support for their families in the future, as well as continuing the family name, whereas a daughter is the ultimate economic burden. According to the UN Population

Fund, as of June 2020, 140 million girls around the world are considered 'missing'.[1] Take a minute to pause on that number. That is twice the size of the UK population.

## The best start in life

My academic research, these stories and the time I spent at the 'Unique Home for Girls' orphanage near my family's hometown in Jalandhar, Punjab, acted as the catalyst for much of my feminist activism and informed what I still fight for today. This issue of son preference is not a faraway problem, it sits in our homes in the diaspora too. Every time we say, 'Let the men eat first.' Every time we force our daughters to do all the house chores whilst the sons sit idly by. Every time we hand out boxes of ladoos when a son is born but tell mothers 'never mind' when their daughter is born. This all builds the same dangerous mindset that must be eradicated within the next generation. We must reach the moment where we celebrate the life of a daughter in the same way we do a son, starting from the minute they are born. The Pink Ladoo Project is promoting just that. They've been encouraging families to celebrate the birth of their daughters by distributing pink ladoos or other sweet treats, to ensure that families are rejoicing in the life of their daughters from the very start. By celebrating our girls from the moment that they enter this world, we are giving them and the rest of the world a very important message – they are loved, and they are important. Mum of two, Nasreen Nupur wrote in *Brown Girl Magazine* that this is precisely why she knew she wanted to name her daughter Aisha, after the Prophet Muhammad's wife. 'This name was the perfect fit as I started my life-long journey of

211

empowering my daughter [. . .] *Bibi* Aisha is one of the most extraordinary and prominent female figures in Islamic history. She was courageous, brilliant and empowering. After the death of Prophet Muhammad, *Bibi* Aisha's role in politics and serving the public further emphasises her influential status.'

Women have been at war politically, socially and economically for too long. So, when I say we ought to be raising all our children as feminists, it means that we will be saving our daughters. It means we will be saving our sons too, from these toxic masculine expectations. It means teaching our children what equality is, and what it should look and feel like. It means believing in their rights to equal opportunities regardless of their gender. It means teaching our children to have respect for others and for themselves. It means learning empathy. It means instilling the confidence to believe in ourselves. I want sons and daughters to be kind and expect kindness to and from every gender. And who wouldn't want that for their children? Patriarchy has been able to continue not only because those in power have means of control, but because we ordinary folk also police one another and reinforce sexist ideals. A quick example – when a father is looking after his own children, that is not 'babysitting', that is parenting.

When Indy and I decide to have babies, I will gladly assure everyone that our baby gremlin is *definitely* his. That means the parenting (not babysitting), is also *definitely* his responsibility. In the words of the late lawyer and jurist Ruth Bader Ginsburg, 'Women will only have true equality when men share with them the responsibility of bringing up the next generation.' It is here that I would like to say that although I've written this chapter predominantly to advise and support current brown mums and future brown mums on how to raise a feminist, every piece of advice here is also directed at fathers, too. Raising a child, the majority of the time, is a two-person job. They even say it takes a village! So to all the brown dads and dads-to-be out there, I hope this chapter also shows you how to be the best dad when raising a brown feminist. I'd also like to add that although I am not a mother yet, I'd like to share what knowledge I've gained from my experiences of raising my four nephews and niece, from educating hundreds of children in schools and community spaces across the country and from listening to the moving and thoughtful stories that brown mums have shared with me.

Before we begin to discuss the tips and tricks for raising the next generation of brown girls, let's first consider what we already know and what we've already established in the book so far. We know marriage is not her only happily ever after. We want her to learn about and love her own body. We've seen the importance of self-education. But what else should we be considering when raising the next generation of brown daughters, and sons for that matter? Is it first important for us to consider the parenting that we grew up with? In Chapter 1, we considered what it was like for our parents and grandparents to parent from a place of fear, rather than a place of comfort. Let's just say we were not the 'I love you' generation, and that inevitably affected us. But before we ridicule our parents for their parenting choices, maybe we should put ourselves in their shoes. It is OK to sometimes be mad at your parents, but we can also feel empathy for them at the same time. 'As children of immigrants, our parents rarely lived with ease. Instead, overproduction, perfection and exhaustion became the currency by which they purchased a livelihood in a country that never claimed them as kin . . .' writes @asiansformentalhealth on Instagram. 'Now we must protect our children from paying the same price.'

Amandeep Soomal, a cognitive behavioural psychotherapist and mummy of one, told me that she felt that 'mothers often think about whether they are able to protect their children from psychological difficulties, and to stop the cycles of intergenerational abuse and trauma within their own generation. They come to see me in therapy wishing only that their children don't ever feel or experience what they do.' Our parents may have been strict with us, they may have been unaffectionate at times, they may have even treated us unjustly, but we need to let go of the resentment and pain. Remember, you don't need to hold any more space for that. Take some time to unpack your own baby bag from your childhood, see what lessons from your parents worked and what didn't, and only repack the helpful bits into your new child's kit. Saima Mir, journalist, author and writer and mum of three, has been trying to find that balance. She told me: 'I want my children to feel able to express their emotions. I was raised to always be stoic, and this was presented as strength. I absolutely do not want my children to inherit that. On the positive side, I was raised with a wonderful sense of family, generosity, and I was steeped in spirituality. I'd love to pass these on to all my children.' This is a beautiful example of how we can let go of the wounds but still hold on to the parts of our culture and identity that bring us joy.

As we become the next wave of brown mothers raising brown children, is it possible to raise brown feminists (both girls and boys) without entirely rejecting our own culture and fitting into what Western feminist standards dictate? Well, of course! I assure you, there is plenty of useful knowledge to be found steeped in ancient traditions, home truths and old remedies (like turmeric and ginger will save you from everything . . .). Seriously though, when raising the next generation of brown women, the outright dismissal of our traditions is not a solution. We can understand our parents' context, learn useful lessons from them, heal, show compassion and move forward, so we can do better for our kids. Our parents' and grandparents' jobs were to make sure we survived. It's now our job to make sure we thrive. According to the Good Childhood Report 2020, research carried out by the Children's Society on young people's well-being and happiness found that for both boys and girls, their highest mean happiness score was associated with their family, followed by friends, school, appearance and schoolwork.[2] This shows that the happiest place in the world for children to be is with us, their family. That's why it's so important we do the best we can for them.

## Life lessons and role models

The first thing I will tell my future daughter to be is brave, not perfect. Most girls, including myself, were told to avoid risk and failure and to play it safe. It's reinforced in our psyche our whole lives, from playing safe on the climbing frame in the park, to choosing a secure job when we're a grown-up, to asking for a pay increase. Unlike boys, who feel more comfortable diving into things headfirst and are often rewarded for it, fearlessness is not in our vocabulary. But that doesn't have to be the language of our daughters. Founder of Girls Who Code, lawyer and civil servant Reshma Saujani, terms this issue the 'bravery deficit'. In her TED talk, she argues that 'the bravery deficit is why women are under-represented in STEM, in C-suites, in boardrooms [...] and pretty much everywhere you look.' So how can we tackle this deficit?

We can start by socializing our girls to be brave, to take risks and to be comfortable with imperfection. Whether that's through words of affirmation every morning, or reminding them how courageous they are every time you see a little fear in their eyes. The idea of not striving for perfection will also re-inforce that they don't need to strive for a level of 'perfection' in their appearance either, because, as we saw in Chapter 5, there is no such thing. It will also help to stop unhealthy behaviours like competing, comparing, and criticizing other girls or women. Reshma has been trying to foster more bravery through her Girls Who Code programme. 'Coding, it's an endless process of trial and error, of trying to get the right command in the right place, with sometimes just a semicolon making the difference between success and failure [...] It requires perseverance. It requires imperfection.' Living with these imperfections and working through them may be something that brown girls, in particular, could benefit from.

Bravery can also be learnt through modelled behaviour. If a girl sees Mummy taking risks, being brave, making mistakes, learning from them and persevering, she'll believe she can too. As well as having Mum and Dad cheering them on, it also helps if the network around them, i.e. the rest of the family, encour-ages this same behaviour. Fostering an environment of bravery over perfection is something I have tried to apply to my poetry workshops over the years. So often, when I'm delivering a ses-sion, when we get to the part of the workshop where the attendees have to start writing their own poems, they freeze.

They may begin to write or type, and then cross it out or erase it. Some sit with a blank page. But when I re-emphasize that they are in a safe environment where it is OK to make mistakes, when I tell them not to worry about adding in every poetic device or trying to make it rhyme perfectly, I see them flourish! Many of them have since gone on to write poetry of their own.

This idea of being brave and taking risks is something that Carol Dweck researched for years in her pioneering work in education, on growth and fixed mindsets. It's something that I first came across when I was teacher training in a secondary school in London. In her groundbreaking book *Mindset: The New Psychology of Success*, she writes: 'What are the consequences of thinking that your intelligence or personality is something you can develop, as opposed to something that is a fixed, deep-seated trait?' A fixed mindset is a belief that intelligence is static. Those with a fixed mindset aim for perfection, and if they don't reach it, they often give up easily, avoid challenges, ignore criticism, and as a result might not reach their full potential.

Conversely, individuals with a growth mindset feel that intelligence can be developed. Their continuous efforts, resilience, and willingness to embrace challenges will provide them with a powerful passion for learning. They will process mistakes or failures, learn from them, correct them or improve on them. With a growth mindset, brown girls won't let failure define them. When I asked seventeen-year-old Laavanya Balaindra, a mentee at The Girls' Network, what were the most important lessons her parents taught her, she said, 'To reach for the stars. My parents have taught me never to give up, and every failure is an experience that makes you a stronger person . . . To try your best even if you don't succeed, as at least you tried instead of throwing away the opportunity.' So how can we foster this type of mindset in the home? Well, we need to praise more widely. Rather than solely praising them for their result in a maths test or being nice to their sibling, praise them for their process of hard work, their focus, their perseverance, rather than just the outcome. By doing this, we will instil greater confidence and greater persistence. If we can create these environments in our homes, as well as in our classrooms, can you imagine the difference it could make for brown girls? This belief that their abilities can grow and improve will provide them with the basic human right to believe in themselves.

This can prove difficult when parents put a lot of pressure on their kids, or give them a check-list of achievements to tick off. This can be an easy trap for new brown parents to fall into. Because of our own lack of opportunities or experiences throughout childhood, we want to make sure our children don't experience the same. We want them to pass every exam and complete every piece of homework with flying colours. Nowadays even that's not enough, so we make them attend every extracurricular club, start their own clubs, make them learn ten different languages, play sports, play grade five in piano – all by the age of ten and all in the hope that they'll attend a top university at the age of eighteen. We micro-manage and hand-hold them through every part of their lives, hovering over them, morphing into the helicopter parent we thought we'd never become! This tells a child that their worth comes from ticking these boxes, and that our approval as parents and our love and affection comes from them meeting our expectations, not from them just being themselves.

I could spot these parents a mile off at parents' evenings. They'd usually come marching in, ready to attack, their child quietly appearing from their shadow. They'd dive straight into asking about their child's grades and performance, often talking about the child as if they were not even there. They'd sometimes belittle them. If I was to say something encouraging about their child, they'd act surprised, doubting that the child had made enough progress. 'Really? She's nothing like that at home.' I wonder why, I'd think to myself . . . To the parents who ask about their child's confidence and kindness in class, the parents who would want to hear what their child loved most about the subject, to the parents who encourage the love for learning – I applaud you.

If a child's schedule is packed from 7 a.m. to 9 p.m. every day of the week, where is the time for rest? For play? For boredom, even? Because even boredom can be a good thing! It allows you to use your imagination, to be creative. It was on boring afternoons that I started writing short stories, possibly kick-starting my career as a writer, or making up a game called 'Advert Maker' with my brother, where we would choose random objects from around the room to advertise and sell. We'd act out the cheesiest American-style sales techniques, fostering our skills in persuasion and marketing. It was also boredom that led me to entice a squirrel into my kitchen with peanuts, building an obstacle course for it around the room with pots and pans. Despite Mum not being very pleased when she walked in (she screamed, grabbed the broom and shooed Mr Squirrel out of the kitchen), and the right telling-off that followed, it did encourage my love for animals! Some of the greatest thinkers and writers of our time have come up with their ideas out of boredom. So, try not to fill every second of the day. Let them be children. Let them play. When I interviewed my sister for this chapter, an amazing mum to my two incredible nephews, there was one thing that she said that really stuck out to me. 'I want them to enjoy their life as a child, and not to grow up too fast. Trust me, there is no rush!' And she's right. Sometimes, when we're so busy preparing them for the world of work, we forget to allow them to just be present in their current world. Let them be children. Let them be bored. Let them be wide-eyed. Let them be creative. Let them play.

The micro-managing, overprotection and overdirection can also hinder our children from self-efficacy. Self-efficacy is having confidence in your convictions. In other words, it teaches our kids that their own choices and actions lead to outcomes, rather than us handing them everything on a plate. The more self-efficacy you have, the more you believe in your own ability to succeed. When it's low, children often become apathetic and demotivated. It means not jumping in to save them every time they make a mistake or find something difficult, which I know is tough. It will mean encouraging them to believe that they have the efficacy, the ability to do it. Brown girls are often never given the confidence in their decision-making. To encourage this self-efficacy in our girls will be revolutionary. People often mistake this type of parenting as strict or militant. If anything, for self-efficacy to flourish, children need positive environments with feelings of autonomy, love, and support and encouragement from family.

A great way to promote self-efficacy is through accountability in the home, and yes, that means chores! I can imagine many parents throwing their heads back and laughing at me for the very suggestion . . . 'Ha! You try and get my thirteen-year-old to make his own bed, let alone take responsibility around the house!' I feel you. But we've got to start somewhere, and the earlier, the better. Tharnika Kamsanathan, also a mentee at The Girls' Network, told me that 'cleaning your room or washing dishes before bed' has been a part of her house rules for as long as she can remember. Doing chores around the house can have major benefits in the long run, and there's science to back that up. The Harvard Grant Study, the longest longitudinal study of humans ever conducted in history (since 1938!), found that according to the 724 high achievers who were part of the study, what people need most in order to be happy and successful in life is first, close relationships, and secondly, a work ethic.[3] That means finding meaning through work and finding you can contribute your efforts to the betterment of yourself and to others. And, yes – that can be through chores in the home. If we excuse children from tasks around the house because we're busy ticking off their childhood check-list, how and when will they learn about responsibility and accountability for their actions? Chores will help them realize that messes don't clean themselves (literally!) and that things get done faster when they are part of a team.

The thing is, though, we brown girls have always been doing the chores, and I mean always! So how come our chore accountability didn't lead to more self-efficacy and empowerment? That's because so often, the cooking, cleaning, laundry and other domestic chores we were taught, and often forced to do, had the underlying message that we were being prepared for marriage. Compare this to our brothers, who would so often be found splayed across the sofa watching Cartoon Network, covered in the orange dust of Wotsit crumbs. They'd get to the age of eighteen thinking that housework is none of their concern and have no idea how to turn on the washing machine, let alone know which compartment is for the fabric softener. It didn't seem fair and still isn't. The solution? Get your sons and daughters to help out around the house, not to prepare them for marriage, but because it will simply make them better people! They will develop a pitch-in mindset in order to help their own little home community.

HR manager and mum of two Zulekha Ahmed tells me that she didn't let these behaviours continue on into her home – 'I am not so keen on enforcing the stereotypical male/female disparity in home life. I encourage my son to do chores, and when my daughter is older, I will encourage the same.' Nasreen, who we heard about earlier, wrote in *Brown Girl Magazine* that as well as empowering her daughter, Aisha, she also taught her son, Aayan, from a young age that 'boys will not be boys.' By teaching our sons to take responsibility in the home, we teach them very important life lessons in accountability that can be applied to other parts of their lives.

The whole 'boys will be boys' rhetoric is dangerous. It can lead to presidents thinking it's OK to 'grab women by the pussy'. When behaviour gets excused in childhood, it can lead to claims of ignorance in later life. We need to get this right with the next generation. Nasreen said that her son 'will be held responsible for his actions and that he is to respect everyone he crosses paths with, especially girls. Aayan may not understand the term feminist, but he knows that he is a part of the "boys supporting girls" tribe. He will continue to be his little sister's biggest cheerleader when my husband and I are not around.' If we don't help our sons to collaborate and be accountable in the family workings, we are doing a disservice to the wonderful, well-rounded men they can be.

## Why voicing their choice matters

Teaching our sons and daughters about accountability will also help children understand another vital life lesson – choice. About yeses and nos. About their bodies. About consent, which we hope will come much, much, much later in life. If we never give our children choices when they are young, they might not be the greatest at making decisions later down the line. We often take this aspect of choice away from them when we are busy ascribing gender roles. I don't really mind what colour you decide to dress your children in, pink, blue, yellow, highlighter green – the point is when they're old enough to start making little choices, let them. Give your girls (and boys) the choice of Barbies and trucks. Ballet and karate. A dress or dungarees. Some days I wanted to play wrestling with my brother's wrestling action figures and some days, I loved to play with my Polly Pocket. There were even days where Barbie would fight WWE's The Undertaker and win. Zulekha tells me that 'some days my daughter wants to wear trainers. Some days she'll choose to wear a nice bow or jewellery. I show her that all these choices are OK.' Zulekha also went on to say, importantly, 'We never force either of our children to hug and kiss family members they don't want to. We are teaching them that this is their choice.'

When my nephew wanted to start ballet, I was worried my brother might stop him, assuming he might jump into Billy-Elliot-Dad-territory. I underestimated him. My nephew attended the lessons and really enjoyed them. It introduced him to the world of dance and over time he realized he enjoyed other types of dance too. In Alison Vale and Victoria Ralfs' book *How to Raise a Feminist*, they give some really sound advice when it comes to situations like this: 'perhaps we should neither discourage nor encourage any interest hotly. See what shows up in their emerging personalities and never say no to anything based on gender. When you see their eyes light up, THEN ramp up your enthusiasm.' My nephew was also very chuffed to hear that Tom Holland, who plays Spiderman in the Marvel Cinematic Universe, also learnt ballet and performed in the West End as Billy Elliot when he was twelve. Top superhero and ballet pro?! My nephew was very impressed! (. . . Can I also add here that I think Tom Holland is the best Spiderman actor, hands down. Don't @ me.)

We can only hope that these positive behaviours and the life lessons we try infusing into our children actually stick. So often children can feel like the Bermuda triangle – information goes in and then just seems to disappear. But we, as the adults in their lives, can try to model the right behaviours. Philippa Perry, author of the Sunday Times No.1 Bestseller *The Book You Wish Your Parents Had Read*, says that one of the best ways we can do this for our children is making sure they feel listened to, understood and empathized with. This can be through encouraging time to talk, especially during our busy schedules, and perhaps even through family meetings. Encouraging time for talking will help our children communicate when they are sad or unhappy or even uncomfortable. Philippa Perry says that 'denying their difficult feelings is sometimes our default option.' Often, we tell children to not make a fuss, we tell our boys to man up and our girls to stop being silly. 'It might feel right to try to belittle, advise, distract or even scold the feelings out of them . . .' she says. Instead, we need to provide them with space to feel heard, and the knowledge their feelings are being taken seriously. This is especially important for brown girls, who, historically, as we saw at the start of the chapter, have been ignored or treated as a burden. Fifteen-year-old Simran Barham, also a Girls' Network mentee from Birmingham, told me that her parents have encouraged her to share 'any concerns or worries straight away and not to hide them.'

Some people worry that this might make their children too sensitive or 'soft', something that immigrant parents do not want their children to be. But you're not making it any worse by acknowledging their feelings, you're just telling them they are valid and that you're there for them. This will all really matter if there are ever times your child is uncomfortable or in danger. You will be their safe place. In my interview with Zulekha, she told me that she tries to make sure 'my daughter's voice is heard, she is the youngest and smallest voice in my household, so we pay extra attention to it.'

Zulekha went on to tell me about the importance of this time for talking, as she has seen 'how the abuse of girls in brown families is so often covered up by families as shame.' She went on to say, 'I know a girl who still sees the predator who preyed on her as a young child. I never want my child to experience this.' And here lies one of the biggest taboos in some brown communities – sexual abuse – an issue so often brushed under the carpet. For years, South Asian families have silenced victims of abuse because of the supposed shame. The predators are even protected, forcing survivors into a code of silence, as found in the 'People don't talk about it: child sexual abuse in ethnic minority communities' report in 2020.[4] We've been protecting the wrong people, we should have been protecting children and the boys and girls that have been silenced. The report suggested that victims experience 'the risk of being cut off from their families and communities could act as a barrier to victims and survivors disclosing abuse.'

The report also found that as well as the shame and stigma leading to a code of silence, cultural stereotypes and racism lead to failures of the institutions and professionals, such as the police or children's social care, in identifying and responding appropriately to the abuse.[5] So if victims can't turn to their families or other services for help, who can they turn to? Until we see these institutions improving their racial literacy and cultural sensitivity, we as a community need to be doing more to support victims. The shushing, shunning and shaming aren't something children should ever have to deal with so let's always encourage open lines of communication with our kids.

## *Let's get talking*

When I interviewed my eldest sister-in-law, aka Phubi, for this chapter, she told me that during her teenage years, 'My parents were not that open with certain life matters, like puberty and relationships etc. But I am a lot more open with my children.' I've seen first-hand how she's trying to build a safe space for my two lovely nephews and incredible niece to share their feelings about anything they need to. And for the benefit of sons and daughters, teach your boys to express their feelings. Like a disease, we've seen how telling men to shut off their emotions can kill. Let your boys and girls know you'll always be there to listen. Expressing feelings, not suppressing them. That's what paediatric health expert Dr W. Thomas Boyce found critical in his work into children's experiences of nature, trauma and adversity. In his research, shortly after California's devasting 1989 Loma Prieta earthquake, children were asked to 'draw the earthquake'.[6] Boyce found that those who depicted the earthquake positively, with images of minor damage and happy families, were more likely to come down with illnesses and infections in the coming weeks. Those who depicted the destruction, their feelings of confusion and fear were more likely to stay healthy. Why? Because they were given a safe space to express, not bottle their emotions up.

Seventeen-year-old Sinthuya Veerasingam from Wembley told me, 'If parents were to be a bit more open, children may feel more comfortable and maybe more honest; I know a lot of girls who lie to their parents about what they do and where they go and with whom.' Providing time for talk also helps with truth-telling. Inevitably, there will be a time in life where they will learn to lie. Most times this will be harmless – 'I didn't eat his chocolate' or 'I forgot to brush my teeth' – but later on in life, when the lies might matter a little more, providing a safe place to talk could make a world of difference. A great lesson that I learnt from my dad was that it is better to not overreact to what your child does or tells you. Not overreacting makes it more likely that you will keep communication lines open. If a child lies or does something wrong, it's always better if they tell you, so try to always be a calm listener and not to overreact at that moment. Feel free to cry, rant and scream to your partner later though, because you might need a place to communicate and vent too!

Time for talking and family meetings is beneficial for the wider family too. It doesn't matter if you're a nuclear family, single-parent family, extended family with an intergenerational household, living with in-laws or not. What really matters is how you all get along, especially in front of your children. They really learn how to say 'please' and 'thank you' when gratitude and respect have been shown to them, or around them. Navrup Kaur, also known as @sikhmum online, told me that she is 'mindful of the language we use around the kids.' She emphasized how we need to model these positive behaviours and relationships, and 'walk the walk, not just talk the talk.' If kids are continuously concerned about their family getting along, how can they feel hopeful and curious about the world? I've seen first-hand how this can negatively impact a child's concentration and how they learn in the classroom. I could see the distant look in a child's eye when there was continuous trouble at home, their flame seemed less ablaze. But like I've told parents in the past, their curiosity and confidence can be mended after times of hardship, by giving them ways to express and release. A survey by the Children's Society asked 30,000 respondents to agree or disagree with the statement – 'Parents getting on well is one of the most important factors in raising happy children'. Of the 20,000 children asked, 70 per cent agreed with the statement. Out of the 10,000 adults surveyed, only 30 per cent of them felt this to be crucial to children's happiness. Interesting that. Maybe it's time we started to listen to what our children are trying to tell us.

These open lines of communication, built through time for talking, will allow parents and children to return to their bedrock, their core, no matter what life throws at them. These are the things that matter to your family the most. Consider how you can imprint 'your story' into this bedrock. Who are we? Where did our family originate from? You know the old saying, 'You've got to know where you've come from to know where you're going'? Navrup, aka @sikhmum, told me she's been teaching her four children why their identity is so important, 'to be proud of who they are, what they look like and where they come from.' Emory University psychologists Robyn Fivush and Marshall Duke created a twenty-question 'Do-You-Know' quiz to study how families pass on their family history to future generations. They found that the kids who could answer 'yes' to most of the questions had higher levels of self-esteem, self-motivation and fewer behaviour problems. Some of the questions included were: 'Do you know how your parents met?' or 'Do you know the source of your name?' and 'Do you know some of the jobs that your parents had when they were young?' With this knowledge, young people feel part of a larger narrative and have a better sense of self. Check out the quiz online and try it with your kids!

Mums, it's incredibly important you tell your daughters, and your sons, *your* story as part of your bedrock. Did you smash a glass ceiling or two? Do you work in a male-dominated field? Tell them about your milestones in life. Tell them how much of a badass their mum is. Show them. Archie Kalyana, a producer at BBC Sport Cricket and mummy of one, told me she has wanted her son, 'to always respect women. To treat women as his equal. I feel that I'm leading by example, working in the male-dominated area of cricket. He is growing up seeing his mum work all over the globe, manage the house, pay the bills and still be his mum.' Tell them about your brown sisters, too. When I have kids someday, I'll definitely be introducing them to my inspirational friends, friends like Dr Meenal Viz, who works for the NHS. During the height of the COVID-19 pandemic, Meenal campaigned for better PPE (personal protective equipment) for her and her colleagues whilst pregnant with her daughter, Radhika. When I asked her what important life lessons she'll be teaching Radhika, she said: 'To never take no for an answer when it comes to the things you care about!'

In Farrah Alexander's book *Raising the Resistance*, written in 2020, she says, 'Don't keep your badass female friends with incredible gender-defying careers a secret, either. Tell your kids about them.' They need to see it to believe it, and that doesn't always have to be on TV screens. It needs to be in real life too. Psychotherapist Amandeep can see how this will benefit her son: 'My son is surrounded by strong women and I don't think the lessons he will learn from us will be actively heard, but will be actively seen. He will see his mother, his grandmothers and his aunts as strong, vocal, confident women who stand for equality, love and compassion. He will see that we work hard and smash our goals and more. He will see us be respected in our relationships. All of these things will create a blueprint for how he will treat us and other women in his life.'

### Laying down a bedrock

In my bedrock, I hope to nurture a love for learning. That's all thanks to my dad. Reading, and a love for reading, were the greatest gifts Dad ever gave me as a child. In a world with screens in every corner, nurturing a passion for print proves difficult. If I was really into a book, I'd hide behind the sofa and read so no one would disturb me, creating my own magical

Narnia. I was in a supermarket the other day and saw a little girl sitting in her pram, engrossed in what looked like a very exciting book! I felt bad for being surprised, but it was just so rare to see young people reading in public these days. However, the National Literacy Trust's Annual Literacy Survey found that during the lockdowns in 2020, young people's enjoyment of reading increased. Children found joy and calm in reading during a time of boredom, confusion and anxiety.

Reading and learning can also be another good opportunity to give your child choices. Dad would inspire me to read history and culture, fiction and adventure, science and numbers. Authors from all over the world. Names that sounded a little like mine, because authors themselves can become extraordinary people in the minds of young children. Saima spoke to me about the benefits of surrounding your child with positive role models in books, as well as on-screen and in person. 'At some point, your child will realize they are brown and will have questions. Introverted children might not say it out loud, but they will show it when they meet someone who looks like them or find a storybook with illustrations they can relate to. My eldest started mentioning these things in nursery – I did not expect the questions to come that early! At seven, I can see he likes seeing brown men [in books and on TV], I think it's his way of seeing where he fits in the world.'

So, let us fill our homes with books, art and knowledge that help them see their place in the world. I shared this sentiment in a tweet once. It said: 'When we have kids someday, I'm going to feel so honoured to raise them in a home full of love for literature and the arts, with books by brown authors on every shelf and artwork by brown artists on every wall.' I'll share the pleasure of reading and learning in my home, in all forms – we'll go to the library, I'll give them space and quiet in the day to read, and we'll take a book or three with us wherever we go. In my interview with Rupinder Kaur, founder of Asian Women MEAN Business (AWMB) and mum of two, something she said really stood out to me: 'I encourage them [her children] to question everything . . . if I don't know the answer, we will seek it out together.' This environment of reading, learning and growing, as individuals and as a family, is truly beautiful.

Mr Indy Hothi recently suggested that he would also put financial literacy in our bedrock. As he is an economist and an accountant, this didn't surprise me, but his explanation made so much sense. Intrigued, I leaned over – 'Tell me more . . .' How to invest, how to budget, how to save, what it might cost to live independently, the difference between owning and renting, how to get a mortgage. He was absolutely right. It's something we don't teach children in schools and something we definitely don't teach young girls. When I asked my sister whether she's spoken to my nephews about financial literacy, she said: 'We're actually quite open in our house about finances.' Often, families avoid discussions about finances like the plague, so I was really happy to see my sister adopt this open, healthy dialogue about money. 'I share my Excel spreadsheet of income and outgoings, so my children are aware of how we manage our money.'

I also asked my Phubi whether she and my brother speak to the kids about financial literacy, and she said 'Yes! So kids should know the value of money and how hard it is to earn and how easy it is to spend.' Preach! Considering that women hold 70–80 per cent of consumer purchasing power in some parts of the world, isn't it about time we taught girls about their economic power? 'Financial literacy is a matter of social justice . . .' Indy said to me. He made me realize that raising a feminist had more dimensions to it than I thought. Financial literacy was a feminist bedrock if ever there was one.

Somewhere in my bedrock, I also want to engrave empathy, so that whenever there is a misunderstanding or someone has been hurt, we open lines of communication. That may require an apology or two, a show of empathy towards the other person before you repair and move forward. You could do something like grab a whiteboard or flipchart and, as a family, write down your family mission statement, your family rules, your bedrock, whatever you want to call it. Remember, it's about your ethics, not aesthetics, so do what feels right for your family and don't worry about what other people might think. Together, decide what your core values are. Any time anyone goes astray, and that includes the grown-ups too, bring them back to the flipchart sheet, which is now neatly framed somewhere in the house, and remind each other of your core mission.

My dad describes these values as the roots of a tree. You plant and nurture these roots with lots of nutrients and good values whilst the children are young, and they'll eventually grow up and form their own branches. But no matter which way the wind blows, the tree will be OK, with its roots still firmly planted in the ground. My dad also said that adults will have to sway with the wind too, in order to keep the tree intact. In an interview with @sikhdad (a popular blog for, you guessed it, Sikh dads), my dad said that a part of parenting is being tolerant. 'The generational difference will always be there, so you have to be willing to adapt to the different age groups in your life. You will have to adjust as you go along. Sometimes you will have to go with whichever way the wind blows; otherwise, the roots will begin to uproot.'

## No such thing as a perfect parent

Parents, remember – you're not alone in this. It takes a village to raise a child, so for your own empowerment and wellbeing, try to build a network of support around you, people who will have an inspiring impact on your brown feminist baby too. We are pack animals, after all. Since the beginning of time, we have had families, tribes, communities to help on the road of parenting. I'll say it again, you're not alone in this. Loneliness, with stigma still attached to it, can affect us all and can feel like a smack in the face. It reminds us that we need company, or we might need a hand. Loneliness can often be triggered during postnatal depression, impacting 10–15 per cent of women, and as we know, with higher rates amongst ethnic minority women. Business owner and lawyer Sabrina Kumar, who we met in Chapter 1, mentioned how women with 'post-natal depression often put on a brave face so their family or friends can't see they're struggling. Even their own partners don't know sometimes.'

This is where strong family ties within Asian communities can help both parents and baby, and importantly, where families should be listening to what mummy and baby might need. Within brown families, there is a family bubble of womanhood that I find uniquely precious. I have seen these close ties in other cultures too. I loved growing up with so many women around me – my mum, my sister, my grandmothers. Later on, this bubble of womanhood grew – I now have two sisters-in-law, and since I got married, my mother-in-law and grandma-in-law, Beeji, who we met in the last chapter, have joined the network. If close family isn't an option, or if you would also like a wider network of support, lean on a brown sisterhood, a parenting support group or a mummies' network. See what your local schools, community centres and libraries have to offer. Amandeep, who we heard from earlier in the chapter, joined the NCT when she became pregnant with her son. 'This group was a lifeline for me, especially in the early days. Every single pregnancy and postnatal symptom was discussed and dissected, validating any worries I had. The women I met are lovely, and despite me living in that town for six years, they were my first real friends.' Amandeep found this despite being 'one of two ethnic minorities in the group.' Other mums also agreed that these parenting networks can be very white-dominated spaces. Archie tells me 'I tried to attend a couple of mum and baby groups but felt that I stuck out like a sore thumb. I just couldn't relate to anyone. Also, no one ever had any interest in football or cricket like me. I felt alienated, especially living in Brighton with no desi friends there.' That's why it's been really positive to see the great work being done by groups like Masala Mommas and Asian Mums Network, providing parenting advice specific to the South Asian diaspora.

Ultimately, Mummy Bear needs to be checking in on her own wellbeing, too. It's OK to ask for support when you need it. I know we are experts in helping and thinking of everyone else before ourselves, but there is a reason why parents have to put on the oxygen mask first. Amandeep said to me that 'the best advice that stands for all mums is, you have to look after yourself in order for you to adequately look after your baby. No one benefits from a Martyr Mum, not you, not others and certainly not your baby. So, eat nutritious meals, sleep when you can, go for walks and meet mums with kids the same age as yours so you can all complain together.' So, Mumma, look after yourself. And let go of any mummy-guilt you might hold when you are doing something for yourself. Rupinder said that it's essential for mums to not 'lose your sense of self. Being a mum is incredible and rewarding, but we are more than mothers – keep your own passions, hobbies and interests. It's so important for children to see their mothers as full human beings pursuing what they love. By doing this, you are showing them that it's acceptable and normal for them to do the same!'

And know this: just by being their mum, you are already the best form of activist, feminist and role model for your baby that there is. Mums have so much power, and maybe that's precisely what terrifies the patriarchy so much . . . Raising the next generation is your activism. 'So much of how your children will change our world is being fostered right now – by *you*. It's an absolutely awe-inspiring power,' says Farrah Alexander. Some may disagree, but just as our bodies are political, money is political, healing is political, culture is political, love is political – so is motherhood. There's an irony in the fact that the word 'mum' comes from the 1560s Middle English verb, to 'be silent' or 'make silent'. It's most likely where the phrase 'mum's the word' comes from. How can we sit back and stay silent when, in the words of Farrah, 'mothering is one of the most influential acts of activism as the future of humanity lies in our children.'

With all the parenting books, social media feeds and opinions on how to raise eco-friendly kids, gluten-free kids, yoga-kids, tech-free kids, and even feminist kids, covering all bases all the time can be exhausting. So cut yourself some slack. It's OK to be figuring it all out as you go along. It's OK to feed them the gulab jamun that your mum sent over. It's OK to feed them freezer food now and again. It's OK that you dressed them as a Disney princess for Halloween. It's OK that you handed them an iPad so that you could take a shower in peace. All parents really want is for their kids to be happy, healthy, good people. And like Dad said, as long as the roots of the tree are strong, no matter which way the wind blows, they'll be OK.

I think I want to end this chapter by saying thank you to my dad, one of the greatest feminists I've ever known. Thank you for helping me understand who I am. For investing in my education, before anything else. Helping me find the squirrel after Mum shooed it outside. Letting me stay up late so that I could read one more chapter. For giving me patience when I was stubborn. For recognizing that being the 'sensitive one' didn't make me weak. For providing me with choices, so that I never felt that I had to fit in just one box. For never punishing me for saying 'no' in the hope that I never feel there's a time I can't say it. You may not have been marching alongside me in my purple 'badass feminist' T-shirt at protests and marches, but you knew your free-spirited feminist daughter was going to need the tools to fight. Thank you for accepting that those tools may dismantle cultural barriers sometimes. Thank you for nicknaming me 'diamond', not in the hope that I would be the prettiest girl in the room, but to remind me that like a diamond, I may be perceived as delicate, but I am in fact one of the hardest substances on earth. And like the Greek origin of the word, adamas, I am invincible.

# CHAPTER 9

# POWER IN THE DIGITAL AGE

*Social Media, Solidarity and Sisterhood*

*Smartphones and all that roaming*
*But we're still not free*
*We're seeing everything in high definition*
*But we still can't see*

**Video killed the radio star**

n May 2016, rapper Azealia Banks accused singer-songwriter Zayn Malik of stealing elements of her 'Chasing Time' music video for his own 'Like I Would' visuals. Like most celebrity arguments these days, the dispute took place over Twitter for the whole world to see. The confrontation got ugly, with Banks calling Malik a 'sand nigga', 'faggot' and 'paki' who was 'only apart [sic] of 1d to draw brown attention'. Banks then turned to Malik's mother, calling her 'a dirty refugee who won't be granted asylum'. Her insults returned to Malik, when she called him a 'curry scented bitch'. Now I am not here to play morality police on what happened during this Twitter exchange. Nor am I here to decide whether Zayn was a copycat, or to judge Banks's use of social media over the years (including videos of her digging up her dead cat . . .). What I am more interested in is what happened in the days which followed. The hashtag '#curryscentedbitch' seemed to have gone viral. And no, not because One Direction fans were swooping in to support their boo, but because the young Asian female diaspora across the globe took ownership of the slur. Despite the phrase being directed at a young Asian man, it was perhaps due to the gendered aspect of the word 'bitch' that images of young brown women were filling up the feeds of Instagram, Twitter and Facebook. For me, the hashtag reminded me of all the many times I was worried that my school blazer would smell of *tarka*. But more importantly, how tired I

241

was of carrying the internalized self-hate that had been with me since I was a teenager. A hate that made me hide and deny the beauties of my culture for too long.

#Curryscentedbitch is just one example amongst many significant moments in the last decade where brown women have used the digital space to explore, examine and express meanings around their identity. As sociologist Dr Trishima Mitra-Kahn suggests: 'The internet has proved to be instrumental for some women's examination, critique, transgression and subversion of the interoperable gender socio-political and cultural scripts that their lives are increasingly subject to and subjectivist by.'[1] This chapter will look at the more complicated networks of race, political economy, and power as they play out in the rhetoric and spaces of the internet. Current scholarship still has very little on the relationship between race, gender and digital communication, except for Lisa Nakamura's work[2] and more recently Safiya Noble in *Algorithms of Oppression*, and those that looked at the impact of the internet on the Arab Spring. But what we will see is how the likes of social media have given marginalized voices – voices which have been muted or ignored for so long – a platform to be heard, to show the world that they will no longer be left invisible.

We've already seen how many brown women felt that they grew up in a world complicit in their erasure when it came to their lived experiences. Our voices, our stories and our histories are barely mentioned in the school textbooks, the storybooks and the TV screens, but now the digital world gives us an opportunity to speak out. For many brown women, it is our chance to say we are here, we exist. No more appropriating, stereotyping or silencing. No one speaking on our behalf, as we've seen brown men do for us, the white man do for us and even white feminists . . .

I've had a love-hate relationship with social media over the years. Still, my poetic and spoken word journey under the moniker Behind the Netra would never have begun without it. It transformed my life. It gave me a way of instantly sharing my story with a global audience. The same goes for other brown women who have become household names, YouTube stars like Lily Singh and Liza Koshy, actresses like Jameela Jamil, social activists like Ash Sarkar. When my first poetry performance went viral, little did I know a new chapter in my life had begun. I could share my words with the world, and they could *actually* make a difference. The reality is that this book may never have come to life without it. The internet acted as my portfolio of evidence, my diary of the work I'd been putting in over the years. I found other inspirational women of colour online fighting against the patriarchy, the systemic forms of oppression, the erasure. I found poets, writers, academics and friends. I didn't have the social capital of powerful allies in influential positions that could get me to the front of the line, on TV screens or on the top of a publisher's desk. All I had were my words, my keyboard, a decent Wi-Fi connection, a mission, and a dream. I knew that it could be powerful. And that power, my power, kept on growing.

## Powerful online communities

Many brown women have noted that through digital media they have learnt so much about themselves and their own identity, things that perhaps schools and even their families never gave them. It has connected women to their history and culture, filling in the gaps in their knowledge. The digital world has provided space to explore individual identity and meaning and foster collective identity, support and networking. For the millennials and Generation Z brown women, the most popular platforms seem to be Instagram, Twitter and TikTok, whereas the older demographic lean more towards Facebook, as well as independent blogs and websites. We've seen brown women's use of Tumblr fluctuate over the years, as has use of the big names like YouTube, Pinterest and Snapchat. Oh yeah, and there were the days of Myspace, which I'm sure we're all eager to forget . . . These platforms have allowed all marginalized women, whether they are women of colour, trans women or non-binary people, to design their own forms of feminism, sometimes even a transnational feminist vision. And as we ride this fourth wave of feminism, we brown women won't be left behind as a footnote. We now have a sense of sisterhood and solidarity, a unique bond that hasn't happened at any other time in human history.

For this final chapter, I wanted you guys to hear from some of those sisters I met along the way. Incredible female-led organizations and networks began online, some of which have been using the digital space to support their cause. First up we're going to hear from Shani Dhanda, the founder and director of the Asian Woman Festival. When I asked her how AWF began, she told me that she was 'searching for an event where I could meet like-minded South Asian Women in my local area in Birmingham. But the only events I could find were either to book your wedding or buy a new sari.' Shani knew she couldn't be the only woman who wanted more than this and was craving community connection. It led to her organizing the UK's, and possibly the world's, first Asian Woman Festival. 'The event attracted over 1,000 people, including attendees from five countries outside of the UK. The festival was a jampacked day of panel talks, workshops, a bazaar, an art exhibition, entertainment and street food,' Shani told me. I had the honour of speaking at the festival, and I felt first-hand how life-changing that connection was.

I asked Shani whether the digital space supported the cause. 'Social media was really key in creating a safe and accessible space for our growing community and promoting our festival activities, because that's where our audience is hanging out. We are now a global community of over 25,000 people who trust us to share their stories, access our support and signposting services and to enjoy the light-hearted moments too.'

Poonam Dhuffer, a wellbeing practitioner and founder of YSM8, has also begun to feel this global reach online. YSM8 is a community platform which provides workshops, talks, coaching and events on all things wellness. 'Yes, mate!' is Poonam's mantra in life, and that vibrant wholesome energy translates into all the wonderful work that she does. Poonam was inspired to start YSM8 because of lack of inclusive representation in the wellness industry. 'I was determined to create a platform which was accessible for all people, regardless of their background or beliefs. Every being is welcome at YSM8 – today and tomorrow.' Poonam really started to feel her global reach after pivoting YSM8 from real-life events to virtual during the 2020 pandemic. 'I hosted meditation classes, workshops and events both on Instagram Live and Zoom for people across the globe, including a family from Bangladesh, a couple from Portland, a group of friends from Berlin and New York, all together in the same space. The internet has allowed me to translate our offering in a safe digital environment.' Cyberspace and these networks gave women like us a 'safe space'. The term safe space was first coined by Sara Evans in 1979, noting that they are sometimes referred to as 'protected spaces', 'havens', 'cultural laboratories' and 'spheres of cultural autonomy'.[3] The internet has provided a space where similar cultural characteristics help bind people together, and it's free.[4] Whether it is truly 'free' is something we'll come back to later.

Sejal Sehmi, the UK editor of *Brown Girl Magazine*, tells me how the digital world plays a huge role in the magazine's reach. 'The ability to have your work shared and retweeted allows for an increased audience, especially where there are specific hashtags and metatags used, which seems to be the popular method of being part of current and hot topics.' Sejal also noted the support it can provide writers of colour. 'Most publications I have written for, be it *BGM*, *Asian Today*, the *Independent* and *Red* magazine, have shared my work on their social media handles and tagged my own Twitter account, which has drawn in followers and readers to take an interest in what else I have covered around the South Asian diaspora.'

Sheetal Mistry and Shirin Shah, co-founders of South Asian Sisters Speak (SASS), told me it 'literally wouldn't be where it is today without the internet!' Both Sheetal and Shirin were eager to create a space where they could find solidarity and connect with a community going through similar experiences of navigating the world as young South Asian women. 'For our first event back in 2017, we created a Twitter page and an Eventbrite and put them out into the digital world – we had no idea what kind of response we'd get, if any. In the end, we had over sixty people attend our first event, and so much enthusiasm and buzz in the room – just from posting on the internet!' They went on to add '. . . a huge percentage of attendees to our events find us through Instagram.' They both agree that social media has meant they've connected with so many incredible brown women that they wouldn't have otherwise. Shirin added, 'These are often people I would have not crossed paths with in my daily life. Some of these have turned into real friendships, others collaborations and support networks.'

Best friends Amani, Kiran, Jasmeen and Tanisha, founders of lifestyle blog *British Bindi*, also feel that 'the internet has been the main power behind our cause!' The ladies also recognized the financial benefits of using digital media to support their work – 'What we love most about the internet is the tools it's now giving us to enable us to create, share and connect without such a heavy cost implication.' Many of these organizations rely solely on voluntary donations or access to funding, so having a way to market their cause to the widest audience possible without burning through the cash can be really beneficial. The four best friends were going through what they call a 'quarter-life crisis' just after graduating from university. 'We had moved back to our hometown, feeling a little struggle to adjust to the next stages of our life.' The team told me about their deep appreciation for the solidarity and sisterhood they have felt online . . . 'We're so grateful for our audience, who feel like sisters in the way they share their thoughts, positivity and worries. We receive messages not only of appreciation but of thoughts, ideas and accountability for our content . . . Just the way sisters have each other's back.'

For the Two-BrownGirls, now known as ForwardCulture,

the inspiration for building their online platform began in 2011. Co-founders Aaminah Patel and Seetal Kaur studied together at university, where they first 'experienced many negative experiences where other South Asian students were ashamed or lacked confidence and pride in their cultural identity.' They are now on a mission to inspire and empower confident and creative brown women, collaborating with diverse artists, activists and creatives and providing workshops to the community. 'The internet has been pivotal in our work . . . A follower from a predominantly white neighbourhood in Australia once messaged us about how our blog made her feel confident and proud of her identity. The meaningful impact and relationships that we've had around the world would have been impossible without the rise of social media . . .'

Co-founder of The Rights Collective, Nishma Jethwa, told me that she and her fellow founder Angeli Vadera were passionate about creating a space which would allow our communities 'to address such concerns using our own voice and language.' They were tired of seeing and experiencing gender-based stereotyping. 'An example of that is how honour crimes, forced marriage and FGM have been co-opted by the state as "brown problems" which they must "save" brown women from,' Nishma explained. 'There was a deep-seated silence about the disempowerment, inequality, trauma and harm faced by South Asian womxn and marginalized folx.' They wanted to provide opportunities to have 'open and honest dialogue'. The 2020 pandemic confined many of their activities, some of which relied on face-to-face meet-ups and workshops, to the virtual space. 'In the end, we actually managed to connect with far more people across the UK and South Asia online than we ever would have been able to do in person.' Nishma also noted the accessibility that digital media provides. 'I think people often feel more at ease just dropping you a DM rather than a formal email.' The Rights Collective also used this as a perfect time to collaborate with other collectives, inviting women and non-binary people from across the South Asian diaspora to submit works on the topic of resilience, for a magazine which was guest-edited by SASS. 'The reach we got online was incredible, and we ended up having a 'zine over eighty pages long!' Nishma told me with pride.

## Finding a voice and using it

As some of these fantastic organizations have clearly proved, these safe spaces can also provide adequate room for discussion around collective action. It is here that many women, including brown women, have first entered their journey into activism and challenging the status quo, both individually and collectively. For a generation which has grown up digitally native, the inter-net has been a powerful tool to make social, cultural and political change worldwide. This consciousness-raising has led to petitions, letters to public servants and leaders, campaigning, fundraising and holding people accountable. It also provides safety from direct violence and geographical freedom.

In the last decade, we have seen women from all back-grounds worldwide using the internet to mobilize their cause, from Alyssa Milano helping 'Me Too', founded by Tarana Burke in 2006 but going viral in 2017, to Gina Martin, who led a social media campaign to make upskirting illegal (and won!). In her TEDx talk, Gina stated that 'social media is the single most democratizing tool we've ever had for social change. It can be harnessed for good by anyone, anytime.' As someone from a working-class background and a political novice, she used digital media to gain 50,000 signatures, with cross-party support that finally led to upskirting being added to the Sexual Offences Act 2003.

We've seen how the legendary rapper M.I.A. has used the internet and her music to highlight the human rights abuses, war crimes, and displacement that Sri Lankan Tamils have faced. The digital world has even inspired some of her lyrics, for example hearing about 'pre-paid wireless' in her most famous song, 'Paper Planes'. (Side note – do any of us remember when M.I.A. performed alongside Jay-Z, T.I., Lil Wayne and Kanye West at the 2009 Grammys whilst nine months pregnant! Bona-fide hustler, making her name – indeed!)

I asked the ladies in this chapter whether they agreed that digital media has helped brown women challenge the status quo. Sheetal and Shirin from SASS emphasized how 'South Asian women are traditionally stereotyped as being shy and submissive, but the use of digital media to share stories, connect with others and be inspired has gone a long way in shattering that perception.' They added, 'We've found our voices, and we're determined to be heard.' The Two-BrownGirls told me how they've been using their platform to highlight brown women's stories which challenge these tired stereotypes. 'Some of the first interviews that we published on our blog were with Saira Hunjan, a celebrity tattooist and fine artist, and actor, songwriter and singer Monica Dogra!' Aaminah and Seetal told me. Shani from the Asian Woman Festival told me how digital media has allowed her to challenge the status quo in a way that was true to her. 'The ability to create your own noise and express your own views without relying on others to do that for you is priceless.' She went on to say, 'As a disability activist, I have had my story sensationalized or taken out of context too many times to remember, when I have relied on others to share my story. So, taking back that control and telling my story on my terms is paramount to me.'

As well as a space to deconstruct, challenge and express, in recent years we've also seen brown communities using this space to provide allyship to other communities in need and to dismantle ongoing biases in the community. A fantastic example of this is the Malikah collective's programme on 'South Asians for Black Lives', aiming to dismantle anti-blackness. Earlier in the book I highlighted other internet campaigns that tackle taboo issues like toxic masculinity, domestic violence or ongoing mental health stigma. Sheetal and Shirin mentioned how 'calling out the problems and prejudices within our community is such a big thing in itself. All it takes is just one post, one blog . . .' It has helped us all see the collective responsibility required to make our society a better place, not only for ourselves but for generations to come.

## The dark side of the online world

But all this power that has arrived with the digital age has also come at a price. For a little while, I felt I could express reflections of my brown cultural identity and participate in my activism safely online. I thought because no one could physically hurt me or say anything to my face that I was safe. Unfortunately, I was very, *very* wrong. What I naively thought a safe and open public sphere for brown women that had catapulted our collective progression was, in fact, now evolving into a commercialized, private, heavily surveilled and dangerous space. I say dangerous because I mean it. I have received messages in my inbox telling me that I should die . . .

Telling me, someone with a history of depression and anxiety, that I should kill myself. Along with a platform on which I could share my voice also came death threats . . . Rape threats . . . Troll attacks . . . Bigotry and misogyny. I would quote some of the messages I've received about 'what would be done to me' if I kept writing about taboo topics, about feminism, about anything, really. But the messages are so disgusting that I can't bring myself to even type them here, knowing my loved ones will read them one day. It would destroy them. It destroyed me for a while . . . Don't be fooled by my fierce feminist feed, sometimes the horrible comments, tweets and DMs hurt. I remember the first time I received a rape threat online; I was too scared to go back on my laptop for weeks. It reminded me that every time we, as women of colour, find a voice or an ounce of power, there will be someone trying to take it from us again. And I don't want to excuse their behaviour as 'just' trolls. Some of these messages are from the kind of person who lives down your street, or sits next to you on the tube. There are people who hate women so much, especially marginalized women who voice their opinions, that they want you to die. It's been enough to force many people of colour to leave the platform entirely.[5] We're left holding a double-edged sword; the same place that gave us empowerment and the freedom to express ourselves is also the thing that can cut us back down.

Women of colour were being mistreated online before they

were ever really on it! There have been examples of this since the outset. As far back as the early nineties, white men in early chatrooms impersonated Asian women to get attention in these new social spaces. This is what Nakamura then coined 'identity tourism'.[6] Fast forward to 2011, when the world learnt that the famous blog *Gay Girl in Damascus* was not Amina Abdallah Arraf at all, but in fact Tom McMaster, a white forty-year-old American living in Scotland.[7] When McMaster was asked what made him think it was OK to appropriate a female, queer Arab identity in this way, he said that as a white American man, no one would listen to his views on Arab politics. The irony! Tom basically saw what it was like to be a woman of colour whose opinion is always silenced. He was being denied attention, so he demanded it, in a queer brown woman's online persona!

And as the years went on, the examples of online hostility and hate towards women have grown, from the abuse female Muslim academics receive online[8] to *The Good Place* star Jameela Jamil, saying online bullying has even brought her 'to a point of near death'.[9] In Chapter 4, we saw how social media platforms tried to silence Rupi Kaur's visual expressions of menstruation. We've seen how women's bodies are censored left, right and centre, whether it's hair, blood or nipples. In recent years, we've seen the use of Islamophobic and right-wing Hindutva rhetoric increasing day by day, as well as multitudes of trolls' accounts appearing and reappearing every day. Even when it comes to the delivery of the news, only 26 per cent of the people in internet news stories and media news 'tweets' are women, according to the Global Media Monitoring Project.[10] Now imagine how much smaller that percentage is for marginalized women. It just goes to show that the internet doesn't really care about us. Ultimately, we're working in a system that's working against us most of the time. It feels like it was not built for us brown women.

These spaces have also become arenas for big money, as social media sites' and tech companies' need for advertising and desire for profit grows. There is also all the scary stuff about data mining and cyber snooping and the use of our personal data as capital, with us having no clue about it. Then there's the kind of behavioural data that can even be used in political campaigning. If Cambridge Analytica showed us anything during the 2016 US presidential campaign and the 2016 Brexit referendum, it's that what we think, say and do online can have a significant impact on society. Every time we click and type and send and swipe, someone is watching – and someone is using that knowledge to make sure that we do more of it – clicking and typing and sending and swiping for someone else's gain. All a bit creepy, I know. So as brown girls, we all have a collective responsibility to try and influence this data where we can by being very careful about the information we do and do not want to give and what we do and do not engage with online.

As I understand, we are yet to have a program or algorithm that can detect sexism, racism, homophobia, transphobia and all kinds of abuse on social media. But maybe the solution isn't technical at all. Perhaps the social media companies need more trained human moderators, something that's not as extreme as censorship, but that protects people from abusive attacks. Maybe this is where education is the key again. Safiya Noble suggests that those working in the field of computer engineering 'are under-exposed to the critical thinking and learning about history and culture afforded by social sciences and humanities in most colleges of engineering nationwide. The lack of a diverse and critically minded workforce on issues of race and gender in Silicon Valley impacts its intellectual output.' That's why I personally think history and sociology should become a compulsory subject in schools and/or universities to improve our knowledge around race and gender issues, but, hey, that's just me. These industries have been majorly scrutinized for their lack of diversity. There seem to be hardly any women of colour at decision-making tables, or many women at all for that matter. Considering that women technically own the internet in the sense that we use social media sites more than men,[11] should we not be more involved in building the companies and platforms of tomorrow?

Until these fields become more inclusive and more effective in protecting their users, it's important that you protect yourself. And I mean that in the same way that women have to protect themselves on the streets. Aaminah and Seetal suggested, 'In the same way that you would protect yourself and create mental and physical support offline, the same should be applied to online interactions.' How you navigate the online world will be entirely up to you, but as Shirin reminded me, 'Your mental and physical health are the most important thing.' I've taken a few steps in recent years to monitor my usage and what I consume. I no longer have any notifications on my phone except for texts or calls, hoping that will reduce the amount that I look at my phone. And it's worked. Since then, I've been using social media as more of a tool than a pastime. Especially when I think about the fact that Sean Parker, one of Facebook's founders, admitted that they knew from the inception they were creating something addictive that exploited 'a vulnerability in human psychology'.[12] Netflix's *The Social Dilemma* documentary woke me the hell up, and reminded me that these social media apps 'want to psycho-logically figure out how to manipulate you as fast as possible'. It's like a drug and is one of the only other industries that calls its customers 'users'. Think about that.

I usually remove all social media from my phone entirely during festive periods too, so that I can feel more present with my family and friends. 'It quietens the noise and gives us space to reflect on the people and voices who actually matter in our lives,' as Aaminah and Seetal also noted. Even whilst writing this book, I came 'offline' entirely from all social media to implement a state of deep concentration free from distractions or interrup-tion so that I could really push my cognitive capability and get into 'deep work'.[13] Through this distraction-free concentration, I also found myself feeling more focused and fulfilled with my work. Some of the best thinkers, scientists and writers of our time were only able to develop their theories and thoughts because they had no distractions, so if I wanted to do this book justice, I knew I had to do the same. Besides regular breaks from social media, I unfollow people who bring me no light or joy or benefit or just give off general bad vibes and energy. I only follow those I feel I can learn from or feel uplifted by. I block people that I don't have time for. Shani agrees: 'Block and remove this negativity from your online space. Don't let this deter you from your goal or purpose to share your story, because you just don't know how many people it could help.' I'm protecting my energy.

Over time, it becomes easier to differentiate which com-ments and messages will encourage open, healthy dialogue about things you care about, and which ones are just someone being a dick. 'Sadly, it is part of the parcel of having an online presence. Once we put ourselves out there in the public domain, we allow ourselves to be open to critics and attacks,' Sejal Sehmi says. 'As an editor, I've learnt how to navigate between what we identify as constructive criticism and a debate vs trolls who are trying to intimidate, and it's my job to protect my team from that but also recognize where there is just a difference of opinion.'

It's also easy to get a little bit lost online, and I mean literally and metaphorically. As Susan Cousins puts it, 'Social media presents a contradiction between freedom to express and portray oneself and the inauthenticity of much of what and who we are portraying.'[14] Ultimately, social media is a filtered reality, and we saw in Chapter 5 how detrimental that can be to your self-esteem. We choose, select and filter who we want to portray ourselves as in the online world, leaving us all to question, is this really me? Maybe, or maybe partially. The same goes for the other people you connect with online. I'm not here to judge whether that's right or wrong, but just that it's something to be aware of when trying to connect with your truest sense of self in the real world. As Sheetal from SASS put it perfectly, 'Be true to who you are. It's so easy to get caught up in what everyone else is posting and talking about – but if it doesn't feel right or authentic to you, it's really not worth it. You'll never please everyone, but people can tell when you're being yourself, and you'll attract those who connect and empathize with your truth.' Try not to lose touch with who you are in the real world when creating who you are online.

In a world where click-bait-worthy news can travel fast and far, the truth can sometimes get left behind, and that allows fake news to thrive. So be critical in how you gather your inform-ation and resources. Diversify your media feeds so that you don't fall into echo chambers telling you information that you already know or what you want to hear. Be careful not to jump on any bandwagon, any hashtag or even any cancel culture trend without really thinking about its purpose, and what that means to you. I ask you to think critically. Do not do yourself a disservice by not considering all the facts, variables and nuances when it comes to trends online. When studying history, I would always tell my students to 'MAC'* any historical source they were given. It's a teaching tool but it's relevant here: think about the motive, audience and context of the source to help determine how useful or reliable it is. The same can be applied to what you see online.

## No app will ever save us

By putting a few of these suggestions in place, perhaps they will allow us to traverse the digital world safely, to continue finding ways to tell our story and find solidarity and sisterhood. But these digital opportunities shouldn't stop us from considering how we can translate more of this in the physical world too. Ultimately, no app, no website, no page will save us from the oppression that we face. It may help us heal, it may help us find solidarity and sisterhood in the struggle, but it can't be the only thing we rely on.

Aaminah and Seetal told me, 'We have also been taking this community spirit offline and meeting with women face to face after connecting with them online. Through our company, ForwardCulture, we are developing more online and offline spaces

---

* [*to MAC*, verb; to assess and evaluate the motive, audience and context (where, when, how) of any source that you read, whether that's in books, magazines, newspapers or online]

as we have done in the past, such as bringing Rupi Kaur to the UK for the first time many years ago, curating sold-out events with partners like South Asian Sisters Speak and running empowerment projects for South Asian students in London.' Poonam has been building this community spirit offline through YSM8's 'Monthly Meets' and 'Supper Club'. She told me that 'It was through my love of supper clubs and sharing stories as a form of self-love and healing that ignited me to create a platform for community care.' The supper clubs consist of beautiful home-cooked vegetarian Punjabi food 'fused with global beats'. These spaces will also continue the fight to make sure that our stories, our experiences, our voices never get erased or muted again.

Poonam's supper clubs remind me that there is something really special about 'food, friendship and conversation', as she so brilliantly puts it. There's a reason why many of the most important conversations in my life – and even in this book – took place over a cup of cha. For me, tea has always provided a sense of calm, and for generations brown women have been having discussions about politics and identity, about motherhood and relationships, about revolutions and change, over cups of tea. For me, tea feels like home. We still need to hold space for that. Let's lean into old traditions because there is still a magical energy that can be found when you meet with someone face to face, when you have group discussions in the same physical environment or when you are simply in the same room as those you find a sense of solidarity with. I felt this at the Asian Woman Festival, I feel it every year at the Asian Women of Achievement Awards, I feel it every time my girlfriends and I meet for a catch-up over, you guessed it, a cup of tea. I feel it when I sit with

Beeji, and she tells me stories of struggle, perseverance and hope. A large number of brown women – elderly women, grandmothers, or those with specific health needs – might not be able to access the digital world in the way that we do. So, we need to involve them in these important moments of dialogue too, because these intergenerational conversations can benefit us all. There is power in human connection, and you can't always translate that online.

Like many faiths, Sikhs believe there is real value in community. We call it *sangat*. Guru Nanak Dev Ji, the founder of the Sikh faith, suggested that this will help individuals in their personal journey towards becoming closer to God, but the principle of sangat also helped reject the caste system, gender inequality and taught about the oneness of humanity. I don't know about you, but for a long time when I was growing up, I sometimes felt this quiet sense of loneliness sitting at the pit of my stomach. I was never sure why that was. But I don't feel that long loneliness anymore. The solution came from the love, compassion and care of community. So, let's continue to build our community online as safely as we can, while continuing to pursue our safe spaces in the real world too, whether that's through some of the amazing grassroots work we've seen in this chapter, whether that's in your workplaces, schools or even in our homes. Having a community, a brown sisterhood, a sense of solidarity reminds you that you are not alone in this. Every time you feel erased, you're not alone. Every time you feel muted, you're not alone. Every time there is a social injustice to fight, you won't be alone. You're reminded that somewhere out there is another brown girl like me.

# DEAR BROWN GIRL
## LIKE ME . . .

There are lots of reasons behind why I decided to write this book
. . . To challenge the existing portrayals of brown women, to
tackle erasure, to share some of our stories. To heal. But ultimately, I was writing down all the things that I wish I could have
told my younger self. So here I am, reaching my hand out to that
teenage girl crying on the bathroom floor . . .

I want to tell her that before you can save the world, tackle
stereotypes and break down barriers, remember that you will
always need to keep saving yourself, first. Healing yourself, first.
Loving yourself, first. That self-compassion and a foundation of
self-love will give you the strength to take on the world.

There will be times when the sting of erasure when you are
young – in literature, in TV or in occupying positions of power
– will feel confusing. You will sometimes grow up feeling lonely,
and even more so in white and/or male-dominated spaces. But
don't forget that a sisterhood exists that can support you. You are
not alone. Talk about your pains, worries and anxieties. Write
them down, speak to someone, share them and never bottle
anything in.

People will make their assumptions about what it means to

be a brown woman. You might be labelled; you might get pigeonholed by societal and cultural expectations. But remember that you, as a brown girl, don't have to fit into one box. Tick all the boxes, tick no boxes, destroy the boxes. And no matter what anyone tells you, your only goal in life isn't just to get married or make babies. Be who you want to be so that you can live a life with passion and purpose.

You have the right to your anger, sadness and fear. You will grow up having to fight people with ignorant non-arguments, people who insist that there is no problem, and you will learn that you can't persuade everyone. But you deserve to be able to speak your truth, and you deserve to be heard. So keep calling out every piece of bullshit that doesn't feel right to you, whether it's political, social or cultural. This might even have to start in your home.

Always continue to educate yourself, and sometimes that will mean outside of the classroom. Understand your own history, your own identity and all that it entails. Read. Keep reading, and as you get older, keep diversifying the books you read. Look. Listen. In this age of digital information, there is no excuse for you to grow up ignorant. But keep in mind that along with the mass of information must also come critical thinking, debate and questioning. And remember, before you expect anyone else to understand your injustices, *you* must understand them first. Learn about who you are.

Take the time to learn about your body too, get to know it, become more familiar with it. Learn to love it like a dear friend even when the world doesn't want you to. Stop defaulting to Western beauty standards or whiteness as the ideal. All bodies, in all their shapes and colours and forms, are beautiful.

You might feel that this fight is too big for you. How on earth can you dismantle so many complex, long-standing systems of oppression? My answer: piece by piece. There are big pieces, and there are small pieces. The way you vote, the way you spend your money, the way you love yourself, and what you do and do not call out will all define the future histories of brown women. And I appreciate that that's a heavy load to bear, so don't feel like you need to fight all of these things, all of the time. Herein lies an important life lesson, to rest, and to find the joy and beauty in the journey too.

Around the country are brown women, incredible role models who are effecting real change through small actions, through wisdom, sisterhood, solidarity, protest and art. Find them. Support them. Grow with them. You can find them online and in person. Some of them might be even closer than you think.

For our societies to become happier, healthier and safer places for brown women to exist in, you will need to teach people to be empathetic. No one is born racist, misogynistic, or full of hate, sadly they have been taught to become that way by society. You can teach them otherwise. And the way to do that is to share your story, share how you feel, who you are, what you've experienced and all your vulnerabilities. Remember what Dad taught you: 'anger will make you strong . . . but love will make you powerful.' Turn that anger into hope and love.

The answers to a lot of the questions in this book and the shape of the world that you will inhabit will not just be determined by the powerful and by those with lots of money, but by thousands of ordinary brown girls, just like you, who choose to love themselves, by those who choose whether or not to engage with difficult issues, by those who decide to try and grasp our own narrative of history and identity and find their place in it, and by those that find their voice and make it heard. So roar, sister, roar.

Keep fighting the good fight,
Jaspreet

# AFTERWORD

Though this book was really and truly seven years in the making, the turn of the decade was when I sat down and told myself to write the book I always hoped had existed. I'd just taken a break from teaching and started my associate research fellow position with an office on Gower Street. Living up my best life. But then, in March 2020, the whole world turned upside down. Indy and I set up a small desk in the corner of our bedroom, with Beeji making *saag* downstairs, the rest of the family competing for Wi-Fi connection, and I began writing this book. Maybe a book for a brown girl like me was never meant to be written at a romantic writer's retreat in the countryside, a cabin in the woods or a fancy office in central London. Maybe I was meant to write this book in the home, one of the most complex arenas that a brown woman has to navigate, but also a haven, a place that holds so many of our stories.

Writing this book in the context of the pandemic made it even more critical. It conveyed the deep-rooted and pervasive structural inequality that women are facing. The World Economic Forum's Global Gender Gap Report 2021 suggested that the impact of the pandemic means the expected closing of the

265

global gender gap has increased by a generation, from 99.5 years in the future to 135.6 years.[1]

Lockdown measures meant more isolation, and sexual and domestic violence against women increased. The gender divide within the home grew, with many brown women experiencing the caring responsibilities falling heavily on them. And then there was the news that minority ethnic groups were two to four times more likely to die of COVID-19 than those among the white population in England.[2] We lost loved ones here in the diaspora and endured the pain of losing loved ones in our homelands too.

From the death of George Floyd to the Indian farmers' protests, we saw some of the largest demonstrations ever seen in human history. There was the murder of Sarah Everard. Historic interviews and impeachments. It felt like we were finally waking up to the reality of the ugly truths hidden in the fabric of our society.

But that fabric can be unwoven and restitched with threads filled with tolerance, justice and humanity. I'm an optimist, so I feel meaningful change is possible. I'm hopeful. To me, the stories of the women in this book show signs of that hope.

# NOTES

## 1. Brown and Down: *Rethinking Mental Health*

1  A. Memon, K.Taylor, L. M. Mohebati et al., 'Perceived barriers to accessing mental health services among black and minority ethnic (BME) communities: a qualitative study in Southeast England', *BMJ Open* 2016;6:e012337. doi:10.1136/bmjopen-2016 012337

2  Karen Newbigging and Manjit Bola, 'Mental wellbeing and Black and minority ethnic communities: conceptual and practical issues', in *Public Mental Health Today*, ed. Isabella Goldie (Pavilion, 2010)

3  P. Fossion, M. C. Rejas, L. Servais, I. Pelc, S. Hirsch, 'Family approach with grandchildren of Holocaust survivors', *American Journal of Psychotherapy* 2003;57(4):519-527. doi:10.1176/appi.psychotherapy.2003.57.4.519

4  Tiny chemical tags are added to or removed from our DNA in response to changes in the environment in which we are living. These tags turn genes on or off, offering a way of adapting to changing conditions without inflicting a more permanent shift in our genomes. https://www.bbc.com/future/article/20190326-what-is-epigenetics

5  M. Gerard Fromm, *Lost in Transmission: Studies of Trauma Across Generations* (Routledge, 2012)

6    Samara Linton, Rianna Walcott, *The Colour of Madness Anthology: exploring BAME mental health in the UK* (Skiddaw Books, 2018), p.iii

7    *Family Matters: Attitudes towards mental health in the South Asian community of Harrow, North West London, Time to Change* (2010)

8    https://www.thecalmzone.net/about-calm/what-is-calm/

9    https://www.un.org/en/sections/issues-depth/ageing/

10   R. Mooney, D. Trivedi, S. Sharma, 'How do people of South Asian origin understand and experience depression? A protocol for a systematic review of qualitative literature', *BMJ Open* 2016;6:e011697. doi: 10.1136/bmjopen-2016-011697

11   G. M. Breakwell (1992), 'Social representations and social identity', *Papers on Social Representations*, 2 (3), retrieved from http://www.psych.lse.ac.uk/Psr/PSR1993/2_1993Brea2.pdf; G. M.Breakwell (2001), 'Mental models and social representations of hazards: the significance of identity processes', *Journal of Risk Research*, 4 (4), 341-351. doi: 10.1080/13669870110062730

12   S. Fenton and A. Sadiq-Sangster (1996), 'Culture, relativism and the expression of mental distress: South Asian women in Britain', *Sociology of Health & Illness*, 18: 66–85. https://doi. org/10.1111/1467-9566.ep10934418

13   The Inquiry Report, *Creative Health: The Arts for Health and Wellbeing – Second Edition* (2017).

14   https://www.apa.org/monitor/jun02/writing

## 2. Beyond the Classroom: *Asian Girls and Education*

1    GCSE results ('Attainment 8'), National Statistics, Department of Education, published 22 August 2019

2    Paul Bagguley and Yasmin Hussain, *The role of higher education in providing opportunities for South Asian women* (Bristol: Joseph Rowntree Foundation by The Policy Press, 2007)

3    According to research conducted by INvolve in March 2018

4    G. Bhatti, *Asian children at home and at school: an ethnographic study* (Routledge, 1999)

5    L. Archer (2008), 'The impossibility of minority ethnic educational
     "success": an examination of the discourses of teachers and
     pupils in British secondary schools', *European Educational
     Research Journal*, 7(1), 89–107. D. Youdell, *Impossible Bodies,
     Impossible Selves: exclusions and student subjectivities* (Dordrecht,
     The Netherlands: Springer, 2006)

6    Schools Pupils and their Characteristics 2019 https://assets.
     publishing.service.gov.uk/government/uploads/system/uploads/
     attachment_data/file/812539/Schools_Pupils_and_their_Character-
     istics_2019_Main_Text.pdf

7    https://www.theguardian.com/us-news/2020/jun/11/only-
     fifth-of-uk-universities-have-said-they-will-decolonise-
     curriculum

8    School Teacher Workforce, National Statistics, Department of
     Education, published 25 June 2020

9    Ibid.

### 3. That's Not My Name: *Managing Microaggressions*

1    https://www.nea.org/advocating-for-change/new-from-nea/
     lasting-impact-mispronouncing-students-names

2    D. W. Sue, C. M. Capodilupo, G. C. Torino, J. M. Bucceri, A. M.
     Holder, K. L. Nadal, M. Esquilin (2007), 'Racial microaggressions
     in everyday life: implications for clinical practice', *American
     Psychologist*, 62 (4): 271–86

3    Kevin L. Nadal et al. (2014), 'The Adverse Impact of Racial
     Microaggressions on College Students' Self-Esteem', *Journal of
     College Student Development*, vol. 55 no. 5, 461–74. Project
     MUSE

4    ONS Ethnicity Pay Gaps in Great Britain: 2018.

5    Ibid.

6    https://coco-net.org/problem-woman-colour-nonprofit-
     organizations/screen-shot-2018-03-08-at-2-03-57-pm/

7    Sonali Patel (2019), 'Brown girls can't be gay: Racism experi-
     enced by queer South Asian women in the Toronto LGBTQ
     community', *Journal of Lesbian Studies*, 23:3, 410–23

8   Susan Cousins, *Overcoming Everyday Racism: Building Resilience and Wellbeing in the Face of Discrimination and Microaggressions* (Jessica Kingsley Publishers, 2019)

### 4. Smashing Shame: *Menstruation and Other Taboos*

1   Plan UK 2018 Report: Break the Barriers: Girls' Experiences of Menstruation in the UK

2   Muhammad Ikhsan, Muhammad Fidel Ganis Siregar, R. Muharam, 'The relationship between Ramadan fasting with menstrual cycle pattern changes in teenagers', *Middle East Fertility Society Journal*, vol. 22, Issue 1, 2017, 43–7, ISSN 1110-5690. https://doi.org/10.1016/j.mefs.2016.08.004

3   Nikky-Guninder Kaur Singh, *The Feminine Principle in the Sikh Vision of the Transcendent* (Cambridge University Press, 1993)

4   https://www.wateraid.org/uk/media/better-toilets-accurate-information-about-periods-crucial-to-keeping-girls-in-school-wateraid

5   https://moderndiplomacy.eu/2018/01/21/shame-stigma-taboo-menstruating-south-asia/

6   Plan UK 2018 Report: Break the Barriers: Girls' Experiences of Menstruation in the UK

7   'What do women say? Reproductive health is a public health issue', Public Health England, published 26 June 2018

8   Nadiya Hussain, *Finding My Voice* (Headline Home, 2019), p.92

9   Gabrielle Jackson, *Pain and Prejudice: A call to arms for women and their bodies* (Piatkus, 2019), p.11

10  https://longreads.com/2019/06/21/yentl-syndrome-a-deadly-data-bias-against-women/

11  M. Knight, K. Bunch, D. Tuffnell et al. (2019), MBRRACE-UK reports | MBRRACE-UK | NPEU. Npeu.ox.ac.uk. https://www.npeu.ox.ac.uk/mbrrace-uk/reports

12  Catherine Griffiths, Audrey Prost and Graham Hart (2008), 'Sexual and reproductive health of South Asians in the UK: An overview', *Journal of Family Planning and Reproductive Health Care*, 34, 251–60

### 5. Ripped Roots: *Brown Bodies, Body Hair and Colourism*

1   Rebecca M. Herzig, *Plucked, The History of Hair Removal* (New York University Press, 2015)

2   Gilbert Powderly Farrar, *The Typography of Advertisements That Pay: How to Choose and Combine Type Faces, Engravings and All the Other Mechanical Elements of Modern Advertisement Construction* (D. Appleton & Company, 1917), p.182

3   https://www.pri.org/stories/2016-09-12/data-hate-crimes-against-muslims-increased-after-911

4   https://www.pri.org/stories/2016-09-23/his-brother-was-murdered-wearing-turban-after-911-last-week-he-spoke-killer

5   Nancy Scheper-Hughes and Margaret M. Lock (1987), 'The Mindful Body: A Prolegomenon to Future Work in Medical Anthropology', *Medical Anthropology Quarterly*, New Series, 1, no. 1, 6–41

6   S. E. Johnson (2002), 'The pot calling the kettle black: Gender-specific health dimensions of color prejudice in India', *Journal of Health Management*, 4, 215–27

7   Aisha Phoenix, 'Colourism and the Politics of Beauty', *Feminist Review* 108, no. 1 (November 2014): 97–105. https://doi.org/10.1057/fr.2014.18

### 6. Sari, Not Sorry: *The Cultural Appropriation Conversation*

1   'Kim' in *The Concise Oxford Companion to English Literature*, eds Margaret Drabble and Jenny Stringer (Oxford University Press, 2007). Oxford Reference Online

2   https://www.independent.co.uk/news/uk/home-news/boris-johnson-muslim-women-letterboxes-burqa-islamphobia-rise-a9088476.html

3   https://metro.co.uk/2019/08/12/teenagers-called-girl-10-terrorist-asked-play-10557754/

### 8. Mum's the Word: *Parenthood and Raising a Brown Feminist*

1   Missing according to feticide (the act of killing a fetus), forced abortion and sterilization, abandonment, adoption, gendercide,

dowry-violence and child trafficking. https://www.unfpa.org/swop

2 https://www.childrenssociety.org.uk/sites/default/files/2020-11/Good-Childhood-Report-2020.pdf

3 https://news.harvard.edu/gazette/story/2017/04/over-nearly-80-years-harvard-study-has-been-showing-how-to-live-a-healthy-and-happy-life/

4 IICSA, 'People don't talk about it: child sexual abuse in ethnic minority communities', June 2020 [Accessed via: https://www.iicsa.org.uk/publications/research/child-sexual-abuse-ethnic-minority-communities]

5 Ibid.

6 W. Thomas Boyce, *The Orchid and the Dandelion: Why Sensitive People Struggle and How All Can Thrive* (Bluebird, 2019)

### 9. Power in the Digital Age: *Social Media, Solidarity and Sisterhood*

1 Trishima Mitra Kahn, 'Offline issues, online lives? The emerging of cyberlife of feminist politics in urban India', in Srila Roy, *New South Asian Feminisms* (Bloomsbury, 2012), p.108

2 She is the author of *Digitizing Race: Visual Cultures of the Internet* (2008), *Cybertypes: Race, Ethnicity, and Identity on the Internet* (2013) and is co-editor of *Race in Cyberspace* (2013)

3 Sara Evans, *Personal Politics: The Roots of Women's Liberation in the Civil Rights Movement and the New Left*

4 'Free Spaces' in Collective Action Author(s): Francesca Polletta Source: *Theory and Society*, vol. 28, No. 1 (Feb. 1999), 1–38

5 https://www.theatlantic.com/technology/archive/2016/07/twitter-swings-the-mighty-ban-hammer/492209/

6 Eds. Jennifer Malkowski and TreaAndrea M. Russworm. Indianapolis, IN: Indiana University Press. L. Nakamura (2005), 'Race In/For Cyberspace: Identity Tourism and Racial Passing on the Internet', *Work and Days,* vol. 13. https://smg.media.mit.edu/library/nakamura1995.html

7 https://www.ibtimes.com/

said-says-amina-hoax-macmaster-mind-orientalist-290801

8   https://journals.sagepub.com/doi/full/10.1177/2056305116678896

9   https://www.independent.co.uk/life-style/jameela-jamil-online-bullying-death-twitter-harassment-triggering-a9353996.html

10  https://pmc.aut.ac.nz/articles/end-sexism-and-invisibility-women-media-3848

11  https://www.statista.com/statistics/274828/gender-distribution-of-active-social-media-users-worldwide-by-platform/

12  https://www.theguardian.com/technology/2017/nov/09/facebook-sean-parker-vulnerability-brain-psychology

13  Cal Newport, *Deep Work*, (Piatkus, 2016)

14  Susan Cousins, *Overcoming Everyday Racism*, p.126

### Afterword

1   https://www.weforum.org/reports/global-gender-gap-report-2021

2   Public Health England, 'Disparities in the risk and outcomes of COVID-19'. https://www.gov.uk/government/publications/covid-19-review-of-disparities-in-risks-and-outcomes

# ACKNOWLEDGEMENTS

Thank you to the team of people who helped me get this book here today. A huge thank you to my dream agent, Florence Rees. I will be forever grateful for you helping me shape a book idea that got me to my very first book auction. Thank you for guiding me through the world of publishing, a world that was so new and confusing to me. Thank you for being so kind and warm during every panicked phone call, the cries but also all the wins! Thank you to my incredible editor Carole Tonkinson for believing in this book just as much as I did. Thank you for asking all the right questions, sharpening my ideas with such detail and thoughtfulness. Also, a massive thank you to the rest of the Bluebird and Pan Macmillan team, Louise, Zainab, Hockley, Jodie, Jess, Katy, Sian and Amy.

Deborah Mabbett, Sarah Childs and Ben Worthy, a special thank you for accepting my writer in residency post as an associate research fellow at Birkbeck's Centre for British Political Life. The access to research and resources has been invaluable. Thank you to my mentor Debbie Gillatt for reminding me to give to myself the same way I give to others. Thank you to the Pathway to Success Programme with Operation Black Vote and Oxford University's Magdalen College and Blavatnik School of Government for pairing me with Debbie and reminding me what it is that I'm fighting for.

A special thank you to The Girls' Network, thank you, Krishna and Claire, for your tremendous support and to the fantastic mentees that were happy for me to interview them for this book. Thanks to Sikh & Dread for capturing the photograph that made it to the front cover and reminding me that I ain't no shy bride! Thanks to my therapist for helping me find my light again and guiding me on my mindfulness journey to heal and be more intentional, present and focused.

I am grateful to the teachers that believed in me and changed my life, teachers like my A-level sociology teacher, Ms McCarthy. Thank you to all the teachers I have worked with and learnt from in my years so far as an educator. I owe so much to all the faculty and fellow students involved in the Gender, Society and Representation MA at UCL for broadening my feminist mission.

I'll always be thankful for the free state education that I received growing up; though it is flawed, I had access to an education when thousands of brown women worldwide can't say the same. Thank you to all the free libraries I went to as a child and as a grown-up. It equipped me with a lot of the tools that I needed.

Thank you to all my students, past and present, for giving me hope, and who taught me so much about the more just world they dreamed of. In the words of Paulo Freire, 'The teacher is no longer merely the-one-who-teaches, but one who is himself taught in dialogue with the students, who in turn while being taught also teach.' Thank you to wonderful intergenerational groups of women that joined my online writing workshops whilst I was writing this book. You uplifted my spirit in indescribable ways when I most needed it.

I'm indebted to the giants on whose shoulders I stand, Amrit Wilson, Arundhati Roy, Srila Roy, the late Nawal El Saadawi, for your groundbreaking work and for making me believe a book like mine was even possible. Thank you to outlets like Gal Dem, *Burnt Roti, Brown Girl Magazine* and the Asian Woman Festival for providing the platform and space for brown women to share their stories in recent years. Thank you to the black and brown feminists, historians, theorists and writers that changed my life, many of whose thoughts and findings have been noted in this book. I owe my fire, grit and passion to them.

Thank you to my girlfriend WhatsApp groups for your continuous moral support and silly memes, and all the lovely friends for being patient and supportive while I disappeared into my writing cave for months. Thank you for getting me out of the house and joining me on dog walks when I felt stuck. Here I should add a special acknowledgement that has to be given to my big ol' doggie, Heera, for our daily walks and cuddles. Thank you for getting me out of bed every day, especially on the darker days I thought I couldn't.

A big thank you to my friends Casey Burchell and Lizzie Exton, your support and feedback have really helped shape the book, especially those very rough first drafts! Thank you to all the friends Indy and I met on our travels in 2017 and 2018. That year shaped my life in so many ways, and it's where Indy and I first started writing the proposal for this book on a campsite in the middle of the Namibian desert.

My deepest gratitude goes to my many families, family by

blood, by marriage and by choice. To my father for always debating with me, pushing me, broadening my horizons and for believing your trouble-making feminist daughter will change the world someday. Thank you to all the women in my family, my mother and my grandmothers, my sister and both my sisters-in-law, whose love and unseen labour is what keeps us all alive. Thank you to Mum for the daily phone calls and Beeji for the cups of tea. Thank you to my three wonderful big siblings for their continuous motivation and for showing pride in their little sister's achievements. Ranz, thanks for the noise-cancelling headphones to help drown out the eclectic sounds that come from living in a brown household. Sukh, thank you for reading every single chapter and sending me back the most heartfelt comments that would make us both cry. My beautiful nephews and niece, for the endless love you give to your favourite auntie, the five of you are my world. Thank you to my late grandfather, Ajit Singh Sangha, for sharing his stories of Punjab and of migration, for setting a foundation for our family. I always said I would write a book with your name in it one day. I'm sorry you didn't get to see it.

The greatest thanks of all goes to my *jaan*, my husband. I wouldn't have had the courage to write this book without you. Your vision for what I could achieve was more than what I saw for myself. You helped me find the confidence to take the leap and write this book. I'll never forget the night you said that we're going to take the road least trodden, and I was terrified. But you helped me see that my mission was bigger than one book, bigger than me. Thank you for the snuggles and snacks during the early mornings and late nights that went into this book. And thank you for holding my hand through one of the most challenging years of our lives. Despite the grief, loss and hardship we've faced, you've helped me find joy and adventure at every turn. We are a team and always will be.

Finally, I will forever be indebted to all the brown women that gave me their time to interview them for this book. Thank you for being vulnerable and sharing experiences and knowledge that I know will change so many lives. To the brown women whose names are seen in this book and to women that shared but want to remain anonymous, I will be forever grateful for your bravery, generosity and kindness. Thank you for taking the wheel and helping me tell our story. Here's to the next chapter.

# INDEX

# Index

# Index

# Index

# Index